Half-Truths

Montague Brown

[signature: Montague Brown]

Half-Truths

What's Right (and What's Wrong)
with the Clichés You and I Live By

SOPHIA INSTITUTE PRESS®
Manchester, New Hampshire

Sophia Institute Press®
Box 5284, Manchester, NH 03108
1-800-888-9344
www.sophiainstitute.com

Library of Congress Cataloging-in-Publication Data
Brown, Montague, 1952-
   Half-truths : what's right (and what's wrong) with the clichés you and I live by / Montague Brown.
       p. cm.
   Includes bibliographical references.
   ISBN 1-928832-63-6 (alk. paper)
   1. Conduct of life — Quotations, maxims, etc.
2. Aphorisms and apothegms — History and criticism.
3. Truth.   I. Title.
BJ1581.2.B717 2003
100—dc21   2003006752

Contrary truths,
that is where we must begin.

Otherwise we understand nothing,
and even at the end of each truth
one must add what one remembers
of the opposite truth.

Pascal
Pensées
Section VIII, 567

Contents

Introduction xi
Aphorisms
Actions speak louder than words .2
All good things come to an end .4
All men are created equal 6
Always follow your conscience .8
Always keep an open mind 10
Am I my brother's keeper? 12
Animals are just as good as we are 14
Be true to yourself 16
Beauty is in the eye of the beholder 18
Believe in yourself 20
Challenge authority 22
Chaos is king 24
Choose the lesser evil 26
Competition breeds success 28
Don't believe a thing he says 30
Don't bite off more than you can chew 32
Don't cast pearls before swine .34
Don't let school get in the way of your education 36
The end justifies the means 38
Everyone else does it 40
Everyone's got a right to his own opinion 42
Everything's determined by the laws of physics 44
Experience is the best teacher 46
Familiarity breeds contempt 48
Foolish consistency is the hobgoblin of little minds 50
A friend in need is a friend indeed 52
Have the courage of your convictions 54

He who hesitates is lost 56

If it ain't broke, don't fix it 58

If they say so, it must be true 60

If you can't beat 'em, join 'em 62

If you've seen one, you've seen them all 64

Ignorance is bliss 66

It could be worse 68

It doesn't matter what you believe,
            so long as you're sincere .70

It's all fate 72

It's better to journey than to arrive 74

It's my life 76

It's not how much you know, but how much you care 78

It's O.K. as long as it doesn't hurt anybody 80

It's the intention that counts 82

Just be yourself 84

Let's just agree to disagree 86

Life is what you make it 88

Live and let live 90

Live for today 92

Look on the bright side 94

Look out for number one 96

Love is blind 98

Love means never having to say you're sorry 100

Make love, not war 102

Might makes right 104

My country, right or wrong 106

Necessity knows no law 108

Nice guys finish last 110

Nothing is good or bad but thinking makes it so 112

One man's heaven is another man's hell 114

Power corrupts 116

The proof is in the pudding 118

Prove it! 120
Read the signs of the times .122
Revenge is sweet 124
Rules are made to be broken 126
Seeing is believing 128
Talk is cheap 130
There's no accounting for taste 132
There's nothing new under the sun 134
Things just look different 136
Think for yourself 138
To err is human 140
Trust your feelings 142
Truth's a matter of perspective 144
Violence never solved anything 146
What is truth? 148
What's done is done 150
Whatever makes you happy .152
What will be, will be 154
When in Rome, do as the Romans do 156
Who's to judge? 158
Why trust reason, anyway? 160
You can only love others
          as much as you love yourself 162
You can't argue with success 164
You can't stand in the way of progress 166
You scratch my back, and I'll scratch yours 168

Persons quoted 171
Biographical note 175

Introduction

We hear them all our lives: aphorisms that sum up bits of life in a nutshell. We hear them from our parents and grandparents; we hear them from our coaches and teachers; we hear them on the radio and on the TV. We even use them ourselves — phrases like "Life is what you make it," "Ignorance is bliss," and "He who hesitates is lost."

These phrases are catchy and easy to remember, and they provide us with quick answers to life's many challenges. We absorb them growing up as we absorb language and culture.

At a certain point, however, they become frustrating. Is it really the case that "It doesn't matter what you believe so long as you're sincere"? Sincerity is good, but what if you're a sincere racist? When you and I close a difficult discussion by saying, "Let's just agree to disagree," have we preserved our friendship or taken a step toward its destruction?

Once I began looking more closely at phrases like these, I found that most of them are two-faced: embedded in them are real solutions, but if we employ them uncritically, they can harm as frequently as they heal.

In fact, questions of truth and goodness can't be adequately answered within the parameters of these clichés we use to guide our actions. They're true in a way, but they don't contain the whole truth. They need to be qualified; and the qualifications sometimes require us to defend what seems to be the opposite claim. Both contain important truths worth preserving.

That fact suggested the format for this book: I've designed it so that it presents you a kind of debate between competing positions. Each left page argues forcefully for the ordinary understanding of the cliché. The right-hand page opposite it introduces qualifications and modifications that must be made if the truth in the cliché is not to be lost amid its error.

Does such debate and refinement give us the whole truth about these issues? Of course not. Truth is inexhaustible. But following the opposing sides in these mini-debates enriches our understanding and helps us think more clearly and critically, which is itself a great help in this time of sound bites and controversy.

In these pages, I've tried first to focus on the usual understanding of each cliché and to draw out the most important corrective to it, but my response is never the final word. More remains to be said. The quotations at the bottom of each page open up the idea to more reflection.

Start reading this book anywhere you want.

Each cliché is its own little bit of wisdom, with roots and branches that reach into many parts of our lives. Not all the clichés ring equally true to all ears. Begin with the ones that sing for you. Then consider others as your interest guides you.

My hope is that consideration of these half-truths — along with their other halves — will inspire you to think, to wonder, and to delight in knowing.

Half-Truths

Actions speak louder than words

The real movers and shakers don't just talk and write; they act. Words without deeds are useless. To matter in this world, you've got to make things happen.

The decisive steps of history turn on the bold actions of men and women. Think of the empire builders: Alexander the Great, Augustus Caesar, Charlemagne, and Napoleon. They didn't simply write about how the world should be: they went out and actually changed the world. Likewise, Susan B. Anthony's actions, not her words, won rights for women.

The same is true in your own life. It's all well and good to talk about what should be done, but be realistic. If you really want things to change, you've got to get involved in the hard work of making your dream a reality. Look at the example of Mother Teresa. She didn't just pray. She helped people with her own hands and heart. That's why she's so impressive.

So if you want to change the world, don't waste time thinking or writing about it. Get out there and do it. *Actions speak louder than words.*

Then I showed again, not in words but in action, that death is something I couldn't care less about, but that my whole concern is not to do anything unjust or impious. That government did not frighten me into wrongdoing.
Socrates
in Plato's *Apology*, 32d

I T'S TRUE THAT great changes in the world have come about because of the extraordinary actions of individuals. Without bold deeds, the world is slow to change. Words and ideas may not bear fruit for centuries, if at all. Without the actions of courageous men and women, civilization stagnates. But aren't all great actions sparked by powerful ideas and strong words?

Did any of the great empire builders act without an overarching idea to guide him? Each had a vision he wanted to make real. Each was moved to act by a dominant idea. And could any of them have gotten men to follow them without inspiring speeches? Each was a great communicator of his ideas.

Think of the powerful documents and speeches that have profoundly affected us. Take the Declaration of Independence for instance. Its opening lines have inspired our nation for over two centuries: "We hold these truths to be self-evident, that all men are created equal." These words have guided us Americans in our efforts to guarantee the rights of all.

Or think of Lincoln's Gettysburg Address. The speech's depth of meaning and the sheer beauty of its language have a permanent place in our national consciousness. The influence of these documents has far exceeded the particular actions of their authors. Words reach a wider audience than actions, and when presented with power and grace, actually inspire actions.

Without deeds to back them, words ring hollow. But without words and ideas to inspire them, noble actions would never see the light of day.

In the life of the human spirit, words are action. The leaders of totalitarian nations understand this very well. The proof is that words are precisely the action for which dissidents in those countries are being persecuted.
Jimmy Carter
at Notre Dame University, 5/22/1977

All good things come to an end

Nothing stays the same. We're bound
to the wheel of time and change.
Every good thing that comes to us
must eventually change or disappear.

It's the nature of the world to change. The planets and stars
are in motion. The wind blows; the weather runs through
its cycles of sun and rain, heat and cold. All living things
are born, grow, and die. Seasons pass. The years go by.
In such a world, we can't expect things to last. The sun
itself is bound for extinction, and with it all life on earth.

Our triumphs are no different. So you've scored the goal
that won the championship? Now it's a new season. Even
permanent things such as knowledge and virtue can't last.
As we get older, we grow senile. Our good actions are
forgotten. Deep friendships weather many changes, but
even they are not immune from death's destruction.

Don't expect anything to last forever.
When things seem best, disaster is
lurking in the wings. It's sad but true:
all good things come to an end.

All lovely things will have an ending,
All lovely things will fade and die,
And youth, that's now so bravely spending,
Will beg a penny by and by.
Conrad Aiken
"All Lovely Things Will Have an Ending"

I T'S TRUE THAT we live in a world of change. Physical change surrounds us. There are changes in living things — birth, growth, and death. Nothing seems to stay the same, not even the good things we treasure. Health, friends, and life all pass away. But if it's true that all good things come to an end, then isn't it the case that at least one good thing — the truth — never ends?

Even to ask this question is to reach out beyond time and change for the answer. And whatever our answer to this question, its truth is not itself subject to change and disintegration. Its truth will not be limited to this place or that, or to this moment or the next. So it is with all truth: it transcends time and space.

There are many examples of this transcendent quality of truth. "2+2=4" has always and will always be true for any mind that thinks about it. That two things equal to a third are equal to each other is another example. Even truths about the changing world are not themselves changing. That dinosaurs are not the same as saber-toothed tigers is true even though both are extinct.

Moral truths also have this transcendent quality. That it's always wrong to kill the innocent, that we should be grateful for good we've received, that courage is better than cowardice: these truths do not change with time and place. And though the physical dimensions of a friendship may be broken by death, the love and virtue at the heart of friendship live on.

> Through changes in environment and fortune, many good things are lost. But truth, justice, and love — which are among the best of things — never come to an end.

And since this standard of all arts is absolutely unchangeable, it is clear that, superior to our minds, which can suffer the mutability of error, there exists the standard of truth.
St. Augustine
On True Religion, 31.56

All men
are created equal

It says so right there in the Declaration
of Independence. Everyone's on an equal
footing. And if we're all equal, then we
all have a right to the same things.

It makes no difference what your gender, race, or ethnic
background is. It doesn't matter how much money you have
or what your social position is. In the eyes of God, we're all
equally valuable. Without this insight, democracy can't
succeed. Government by the people makes no sense unless all
people have an equal right to say how they should be ruled.

This is the foundation of the Constitution and our laws.
There must be no prejudice, no favoritism. As citizens of
the United States, we have equal rights to fair treatment
and opportunity. There must be a presumption of innocence.
Everyone is innocent until proven guilty. And since we're all
equal, we deserve the same economic and social benefits.

Equality is the cornerstone of our democracy. On it depends the possibility of a
free and orderly society. Whatever our
differences, *all men are created equal.*

We hold these truths to be self-evident, that all
men are created equal, that they are endowed by
their Creator with certain unalienable rights.
Thomas Jefferson
Declaration of Independence

I T'S TRUE THAT we're all equally human and equal before the law. The notion that one race or ethnic group is more human than another is absurd. And the idea that our laws should arbitrarily favor some citizens over others violates the Declaration of Independence and our Constitution. But does the ideal of equality require us to treat those who are unequal as equals?

It's obvious that we're not all equal in intelligence or talent, nor do we all work as hard or have the same success. Does the ideal of equality require us to ignore these differences when it comes to rewarding excellence? Or is it not, perhaps, a violation of equality to treat unequals as equals?

It's obvious that in some cases such a procedure is unfair. If you work for 40 hours and I only work for 20, it's not fair to pay me as much as you. Or if you work harder than I do for the same amount of time, it's not fair to pay us equal wages. So also, it's unfair to honor the soldier who runs from battle equally with the soldier who stays and fights courageously.

Not only is it unfair to treat unequals as equals; it's also counterproductive. Business achievements, intellectual pursuits, and artistic creation all suffer if mediocrity and excellence are rewarded equally. Moral character suffers in a society indifferent to the superiority of virtue over vice. Better pay for better work; greater recognition for greater excellence — this is equality.

> *That all men are created equal guarantees them equal opportunity under law; but to reward unequal talent, effort, and success with equal recognition creates inequality.*

Quarrels and accusations arise when those who are unequal possess or are given equal parts. All men agree that what is just in distribution should be according to merit.
Aristotle
Nicomachean Ethics, V, 6

Always follow your conscience

"Do this, do that." I hear it from my parents. I hear it from my teachers. Everybody tells me what to do. In the end, I have to do what I think is right.

Even if I did want to follow the rules, which ones should I follow? Individuals, religions, and even nations often disagree about what should be done. I'm still going to have to choose which rules to follow. What's more, not all situations are covered by ready-made rules. And I often have to decide what to do on my own simply because there's nobody around to ask.

Besides, consider the alternative. If I decide not to follow my conscience, then I do what I think I should not do. That doesn't make any sense. I might as well simply act irrationally. My conscience tells me what's good and what's bad and how I can best do what's right in any particular situation. If I don't follow it, I give up trying to be good.

I have to make my own decisions. If I go against my conscience, I do what I think is evil. That's certainly wrong. It's clear: no matter what happens, *always follow your conscience.*

The eternal laws of nature exist. For the wise man they take the place of positive law; they are written in his heart by conscience and reason. Let him obey them and be free.
Jean-Jacques Rousseau
Emile, V

I T'S TRUE THAT doing what's right requires that you do more than blindly follow rules. Sometimes one set of rules conflicts with another. When this happens, you do have to make up your own mind. And, as you say, you should never do what you think is wrong. But are you really ready to claim that, as long as you follow your conscience, you're always right?

What if you've grown up in a culture that thinks all others are inferior? Your conscience might not bother you if you treated people of other cultures unfairly. Would you be right? What if someone's been brought up among thieves and liars? He might think stealing and lying are permissible. Would he be right?

Since none of us has been brought up perfectly, we all have imperfections in the way our consciences have been formed. We all accept certain wrong actions as reasonable when they aren't: maybe it's lying to your mother or being cruel to the nerd at school. The question is whether what we take to be right is always really right. We need to try to find out.

Since I know I'm imperfect, I can't safely rely on my conscience in its present state; I've got to strive to be a better person than I am now. I've got to educate or inform my conscience. This means thinking carefully about what I should do. It means seeking advice from those who are wiser than I am. And it means trying to get all the relevant facts about moral issues.

You should do what you think is right, but you should also try to discover what really is right. In short, always follow an informed conscience.

If the reason or conscience is mistaken through voluntary error, either directly wished or tolerated by negligence, then such an error does not absolve the will from blame.
St. Thomas Aquinas
Summa Theologica I-II, 19, 6

Always keep an open mind

Don't close yourself off from reality. Don't close yourself off from other people. Do yourself and others a favor: be open-minded.

Can you learn without an open mind? If there's no opening, nothing can get in. Without being open-minded about other people, you can't expand your cultural horizons. If you think you know everything about right and wrong, you can't grow in moral wisdom. Without experiment, you can't gain scientific knowledge about the world. You've got to be open to reality.

Not only does a closed mind keep you ignorant; it also leads to prejudice and injustice toward others. Nobody does things just the way you do. Why should they? There's no reason to think that your way ought to be the standard for everyone. You could be wrong. Learn from others. You don't have the wisdom or the right to close down human options.

So be open-minded in all you do, in your studies, in your relationships with others, and in your morality. It's the only sure way to be truly alive. *Always keep an open mind.*

A man should hear all parts ere he judge any.
John Heywood
Proverbs, I, 13

I T'S TRUE THAT close-mindedness is an evil. It interferes with learning. It leads to intellectual and moral stagnation. It invites prejudice, which poisons personal relationships. We have to avoid self-satisfaction and welcome what's new, even when it challenges us to change our ways. But does open-mindedness mean we close our eyes to conclusive evidence?

Evidence proves some ideas to be mistaken. The claim that water is heavier than lead is disproven by a simple experiment: drop lead into a glass of water. Is it close-minded to accept this conclusion? On the contrary, wouldn't the refusal to accept such evidence be an example of close-mindedness?

So being open-minded can't mean accepting all opinions as equally true, for sometimes they contradict each other. If one says the universe is expanding and the other that it's shrinking, they can't both be right. We must be discriminating, tuning in to the best available evidence. This is how science progresses. Among conflicting evidences, the good scientist accepts the best.

Moral reasoning works the same way. Among conflicting opinions, choose the best. Some think that to make a political point, killing innocent people is permissible; others don't. But you and I are certain that we shouldn't be killed for someone else's point. So why should anyone else? They shouldn't. Only a fixed ideology, closed to the evidence, could fail to see this.

> *Don't let open-mindedness become empty-mindedness. Where the evidence is conclusive, don't refuse to accept it. Always keep an open mind — a mind open to evidence.*

The object of opening the mind, as of opening the mouth, is to shut it again on something solid.
G. K. Chesterton
Autobiography

Am I my brother's keeper?

I can't help everyone — that's impossible. So how can you expect me to be my brother's keeper? It's enough for me to help myself and not hurt other people.

Society is much better off when people just take care of themselves. In capitalist democracies, where it's every man for himself, there's more for everybody. The communist ideal of forcing everyone to share and share alike was a disaster. The Soviet Union went broke because of it; now the people are poorer than ever. You can't force people to be generous.

Besides, it would be patronizing for me to take care of other people. I'd be treating them as children incapable of leading their own lives. Who am I to think that I know what's best for them, anyway? Freedom is the heart of human dignity. Helping others takes away their freedom and hurts them in the long run. They become lazy and dependent; they lose their creativity.

We're born to be free. Only when everyone exercises this freedom will my brother be able to stand on his own feet. *Am I my brother's keeper?* Of course not.

If civilization is to survive, it is the morality of altruism that men have to reject.
Ayn Rand
Time Magazine, 2/29/1960

I T'S TRUE THAT we have no strict obligation to help everyone. Since we don't have the resources to do it, we can't be obliged to. Often, helping others does make them dependent, compromises their freedom, and makes it harder for them to lead a fulfilling human life. But can I refuse to help someone who is in dire need if I'm the only one who can help him?

Suppose I'm walking on a deserted beach and I come across a small child face down in a tide-pool, struggling to get out? Can I walk on by? Given that I can easily save the child and that I'm the only one who can, don't I have an obligation to help her out, even though her distress isn't my fault?

Our obligations to most people are slight. We shouldn't hurt them, but we don't have to be always helping them, either. Our obligations are greater to those who are closer to us in social relation or time and place. In some situations, like the one above, our obligation to help those close to us approaches the level of the absolute obligation we have not to hurt them.

What about all the people in between? How much are we obligated to help them? There's no fixed answer to this question. If someone is stuck in a ditch and I happen to come along, I should help. If someone needs advice, I should be willing to share what knowledge I have. What's clear is that we should use our talents to help others as well as ourselves.

> *Although everyone is my brother in a way,*
> *I'm not obligated to all alike. The greater his*
> *need and the easier it is for me to help, the*
> *more I must be my brother's keeper.*

Men were brought into existence for the sake
of men that they might do one another good.
Cicero
On Moral Duties, I, 7

Animals are just as good as we are

What gives you the right to set yourself up as superior to other animals? We're no better than they are. We're worse — we're the only species that tries to destroy itself.

Animals have interests, too. They respond to the environment like we do. Look how they shy away from pain and danger. They don't want to die. They have families, and they care for their young. The higher mammals in particular are like us. They play together, they work together, and they plan ahead. They have as much right to live and prosper as we do.

In fact, there's a lot to be said for animals being better than human beings. Wars, torture, slavery, indiscriminate killing — these are all human acts. The only real moral evil in the world is the evil we humans do. Animals don't intentionally hurt anyone. They just live according to their instincts, in harmony with nature. So how can you say we're better than they are?

It's mere prejudice to place humans above the other animals. All animals experience pleasure and pain; all animals have interests. *Animals are just as good as we are.*

Those whom we are so fond of referring to as the "lower animals" reason very little. Now I beg you to observe that those beings rarely make a mistake, while we —!
C. S. Peirce
Collected Papers, I

I T'S TRUE THAT we have a lot in common with higher animals. They respond to pleasure and pain from their environment like we do. Like us, they have children and nurture them with care. They play together and cooperate in social groups. They are intelligent and are able to learn. But if they're just like us, why don't we hold them responsible for their actions?

No one seriously thinks we should put animals on trial for stealing or killing. They don't have freedom of choice, so they're not responsible for what they do. Our freedom of choice distinguishes us radically from the other animals. We can determine our own actions and create something new.

Although animals have some intelligence, they lack the ability to transcend their environmental and instinctual conditions. They don't read or write books. They don't study mathematics or seek the ultimate scientific and philosophical principles of reality. We humans aren't limited to our environment: through understanding, we expand our horizons to include all things.

It's certainly a scandal that we, who know better, don't always do what's right. We lie, cheat, rape, and kill, and generally make the world a dangerous place. Animals don't have this capacity for moral evil. In this sense, they're less bad than we. But neither do they have the capacity to strive for justice, to show mercy, or to forgive; and in that way, they're less good.

> In fulfilling their natural capacities, animals
> are just as good as we are, or even better.
> But our natural capacities — to know and to
> love — far surpass the capacities of animals.

The most accomplished monkey cannot draw a monkey,
this too only man can do; just as it is also only man who
regards his ability to do this as a distinct merit.
Georg Christoph Lichtenberg
Aphorisms

Be true
to yourself

Whatever you do, don't betray yourself.
All sorts of things and people will make
demands on you. But never lose your
focus. Always be loyal to the real you.

No one has a blueprint for the perfect way to live, especially
not the perfect way for you to live. You're the only one who
knows who you are and what you have to do. Think about your
options, and choose carefully. But once you've chosen, don't
let the expectations of others push you around. Life's simply
too short to worry about how your actions affect others.

The world really needs this kind of honesty and unwavering
commitment. We don't all agree about how life should be
lived. We're not the same person. But if we'll just act from
deep conviction, laying our cards on the table for all to see,
we might find the harmony of mutual respect and toleration
that we so desperately desire. Try it — it's our only chance.

Don't second-guess yourself. You know what's
best for you. You understand where you're
coming from and you see where you
should be going. *Be true to yourself.*

This above all: to thy own self be true,
And it must follow, as night the day,
Thou canst not be false to any man.
William Shakespeare
Hamlet, Act 1, Sc. 3

I'S TRUE THAT without loyalty to yourself and to your aspirations, you'll never grow in either self-knowledge or the knowledge of how to live with others. The alternative to such loyalty — being false to yourself — is clearly indefensible. Self-deceit and hypocrisy hurt you and undermine your relations with others. But what if the self to which you're loyal is ignorant or evil?

What if you're misinformed about something important? Shouldn't you try to correct this? What if you've made dumb choices? Should you stick by them through thick and thin? If you do, won't things get thin pretty quickly and stay that way? What if your actions hurt people? Should you continue them?

It seems counterproductive to be true to yourself if you're misinformed. After all, the purpose of being true to yourself is to benefit yourself. But if you're ignorant of what's really in your interest, how can you benefit yourself? It makes sense to find out what kind of person you really want to be and how to become that person. This means overcoming your present ignorance.

And unless we're virtuous, how does having all of us be true to ourselves help the world? To be honestly rude to each other doesn't seem very good. Sure, hypocrisy is bad, but it's not the only alternative to rudeness: we could try to care about each other more genuinely. But doing this is striving to be true to an ideal of moral excellence that we haven't yet reached.

> *To be true to yourself is to believe that who you are and what you do matters. But don't be satisfied with yourself as you are. Be true to that better self you can become.*

People often say that this or that person has not yet found himself. But the self is not something one finds, it is something one creates.
Thomas Szasz
The Second Sin

Beauty is in the eye of the beholder

If anything's just a matter of personal taste, it's beauty. What's the point of even talking about it? Beauty is simply subjective. It's whatever you like.

I like rap; you like Mozart. You like Shakespeare; I like soaps. Even those with taste disagree about what's beautiful. Some think Rembrandt the best; others prefer Picasso. Some like Milton more than Hemingway; others think Hemingway's the best. Who's right and who's wrong? No one. It's just a matter of subjective opinion based on what you happen to enjoy.

Even cultures disagree about what's beautiful. Chinese music sounds funny to us; but ours probably sounds just as funny to them. We may have our paradigms and masters of art, but the tribes of east Africa have different ones. As for beauty in nature, that depends on where you're brought up. Some like deserts, others rain forests. We just like what we're used to.

So there's no use arguing about what's beautiful. The reason we disagree about beauty is that it's purely subjective. *Beauty is in the eye of the beholder.*

Nothing is so conditional as our feeling for the beautiful. Anyone who tried to divorce it from man's pleasure in himself would find the ground give way beneath him.
Friedrich Wilhelm Nietzsche
Twilight of the Idols

I T'S TRUE THAT not everybody finds the same things beautiful. Disagreements about beauty spring from differences in generations and cultures. Even within the same generation or culture, people often don't agree about what's beautiful. It's hard to say who's right. But if beauty's completely subjective, why is there, in fact, so much agreement about beauty in nature?

Think of a natural landscape. Whether it's a desert or a rain forest, no one considers a landscape disfigured by bombing or strip-mining as beautiful as the same landscape before it was disfigured. There's broad agreement here, enough to show that beauty is not just something imposed by the individual.

Or consider examples from the realm of living things. Who doesn't appreciate the beauty of a butterfly in flight? The bright colors and bold markings of the wings, the easy motion through the air: these are delightful. And who doesn't find a running horse a wonder to behold? The graceful, rhythmic strides, the perfect coordination of parts: how satisfying to see!

Although there's less universal agreement about artistic beauty, we don't ever really think that artistic beauty is merely subjective. When we recognize something as beautiful, we want to share it with others. And we're surprised if they don't agree with our judgments, and we give them reasons why they should. Why do this if beauty is merely personal preference?

Although the eye beholds beauty, it does not behold it as its own invention. We discover beauty in the order and harmony of nature, and we come to appreciate it in works of art.

Love is the difficult realisation that something other than oneself is real. Love, and so art and morals, is the discovery of reality.
Iris Murdoch
"The Sublime and the Good"

Believe in yourself

Don't let other people tell you what you can do. You're the only one who really knows you. You know your talents, your hopes, your dreams. Trust yourself.

Life is full of challenges. If you're going to meet them and be successful, you've got to have confidence. If you're ever going to make the soccer team, you have to believe you can do it. If you're full of self-doubt, there's no way you'll succeed. This is true of all your efforts. If you want to get promoted at work, you've got to believe that you're worthy of it and show it.

On a deeper level, you've got to believe that you matter. Life gets hard, and it may seem that you just can't make the grade. But every human being is equally valuable. You're just as important in the ultimate scheme of things as anyone else. So don't look at yourself through the eyes of other people. See yourself for the good that's in you. Never give up on yourself.

Don't let insecurities and self-doubts keep you from getting what you want out of life. Remember your unique worth. *Believe in yourself.*

Without self-confidence we are babes in cradles.
And how can we generate this imponderable
quality, which is yet so valuable, most quickly?
By thinking other people as inferior to oneself.
Virginia Woolf
A Room of One's Own, Ch. 2

I T'S TRUE THAT belief in yourself is crucial for facing life's challenges. Whatever you do, you must never forget the intrinsic value of every human being, yourself included. And without confidence, you just can't do your best. Self-doubt can defeat even the greatest talent. But can it be worth believing in a self that doesn't believe in something beyond itself?

The danger in believing in yourself is that you may think you're perfect the way you are. You may be satisfied with yourself in your present state. If this happens playing a sport, you won't improve and so will fail to make the team. If it happens in your work, you won't achieve the promotion you seek.

Of course, your worth is not tied to whether or not you make the team or get the promotion. There are far more important things in life, like learning to be wise and just. Everybody can do this, but that doesn't make it easy. Becoming wise and just is hard work. You don't get there simply by believing in your potential. Such belief can actually be a hindrance to action.

If the self were a finished product, which had fully developed its talents and achieved all its goals, then it would be fully worthy of belief. As it is, we're all works in progress, never perfect. But you can't have progress without something for which to strive. So belief in ourselves must also mean believing in things beyond ourselves — things such as truth and love.

Of course, you've got to believe in yourself.
But to believe in yourself is really to believe in
your potential. To reach that potential, you've
got to believe in things above yourself.

Ideals are like stars; you will not succeed in touching
them with your hands. But like the seafaring man on
the desert of waters, you choose them as your guides,
and following them you will reach your destiny.
Carl Schurz
Speech, 4/18/1859

Challenge authority

Don't believe what you hear from those in power. It's in their interest to have you believe them. Don't just do what they want; stand up for your own interests.

There's no progress without challenging authority. Think of the advances in science. If Copernicus and Galileo hadn't challenged the authorities who said the earth is at the center of the universe, we'd still be in the dark ages. If Darwin hadn't been willing to buck the tide with his theory of evolution, we'd still be living under the illusion of creationism.

Political progress also comes from challenging authority. Only by challenging the authority of kings could democracy be established. If women hadn't resolved to challenge the patriarchal establishment, they'd never have won the right to vote. Think of the civil rights movement. Only by challenging the authority of cultural bias were blacks able to gain equal rights.

You owe it to yourself and to society to challenge the status quo. Don't just follow the herd. Be courageous. Step up and *challenge authority.*

The authority wielded by teachers is often a real hindrance to those who want to learn. Students fail to use their own judgment and rely on the opinions of their master to settle issues.
Cicero
De Natura Deorum, I, 5

IT'S TRUE THAT blind obedience to authority slows progress and endangers individuals and the community. Breakthroughs come about because someone questions the status quo. Moral and political reforms require a refashioning of prevailing norms. There are many authorities that should be challenged. But by what authority do you challenge authority?

Your claim that you should challenge authority implies that you have a right and an obligation to do so. But what's the source of that right? Is it merely personal? Are you an authority just because you say you are? If so, you sound like the kind of arbitrary authority you're challenging.

For us to make progress in any field, we must accept some authority. For scientific progress, it's the authority of the world as it really is. This is certainly not an arbitrary authority; for if science claims to be an understanding of the world and not just abstract speculation, it makes perfect sense to gauge the truth of our theories by the way the world really is.

Moral challenges to authority require the authority of justice. It was right to challenge the authority that permitted slavery, because slavery is unjust. And challenging authorities that discriminate because of gender or race is right because such discrimination is unjust. But if it's not clear that the authority is unjust, we should take care lest our challenge be unjust.

By all means challenge authority, but not arbitrarily. And when you challenge authority, make sure you have the authority to make that challenge.

Those who would combat general authority with particular opinion, must first establish themselves a reputation of understanding better than other men.
John Dryden
"Heroic Poetry and Heroic License"

Chaos
is king

Things just happen. There's no rhyme or reason, no master plan. No one is in charge. The patterns we see are only accidental products of matter in motion.

Everything has evolved by chance. There was an initial burst of energy — what we call the Big Bang. After that, there were random interactions of energized matter. These eventually evolved by chance into the present state of things. This blind evolution has to be true. Stars and gases don't think or plan. Obviously, there weren't any intelligent agents to guide things.

Sure, it looks like things are the result of a plan. There does seem to be a lot of order in the universe, more than what you'd expect from mere chance. But this is just an illusion. There's no plan. The apparent order of things is just the result of billions and billions of accidental interactions. Of the many statistical possibilities, this is the world that turned up.

The world looks ordered, but it's not.
Clearly, you can't get more from less.
If you start with randomness,
you end with it. *Chaos is king.*

The human understanding is of its own nature prone to suppose the existence of more order and regularity in the world than it finds.
Francis Bacon
The New Organon, Aphorism 45

IT'S TRUE THAT we can't penetrate scientifically to the beginning of the universe. Everything seems to have come from a burst of energy that can't be explained. If the initiation of the universe was random, any development that followed has also been random. But if everything is random, isn't your judgment that everything is random itself just random?

If what you say is true, then like everything else, human thoughts are products of chance. They're no less random than anything else. All your thoughts (and mine) are in vain. If everything's a matter of chance, chances are we wouldn't be talking about it; and if we are, we're wasting our time.

Nor could we have any reason to believe in free choice and deliberate action. If our choices are random events, then they're in no real sense ours. We don't control our actions; we don't deliberate about them; we're not their source. You're not free to present what you think is true to me, and I'm not free to agree or disagree with you. Our actions are absurd.

If, on the other hand, we do communicate with each other, and if we are responsible in some sense for our actions, then everything can't be just a matter of chance. If activities such as my writing this sentence and your reading it are meaningful at all, then chaos is not king. Understanding is an act of order not disorder; free choice is an act of purpose, not randomness.

> *There is much that we don't know and can't control. But every time we understand something or freely choose, we reign over chaos.*

Whence arises all that order and beauty which we see in the world? How came the bodies of animals to be contrived with so much art?
Isaac Newton
Optics, III, 1

Choose
the lesser evil

When you have to choose between
bad things, always choose the lesser
evil. It's obvious. The alternative is to
choose the greater evil, which is absurd.

It's the way we normally act when we're in trouble. As you
fall off your bike, you stick out your hand. It's not that you
want to skin your palm, but that's better than hitting your
head. If you can't study enough for two exams, you study for
the one that's more important. When ill, you choose the pain of
surgery rather than the greater evil of long-term pain or death.

Morally, it's no different. We don't normally think stealing food
is good, but if it's the only way to stay alive, we accept it. The
same is true with killing. Who thinks that killing is good? But
if I'm told to kill one innocent person or a hundred will die,
I have to do it. The alternative is to choose the greater evil
of a hundred deaths. One death is better than a hundred.

You're going to run into no-win situations
in your life. Sometimes whichever way
you go, you lose. At those times, you
should *always choose the lesser evil*.

Of the two evils, the lesser is
always to be chosen.
Thomas à Kempis
The Imitation of Christ, Bk. 3, Ch. 12, Sect. 2

I T'S TRUE THAT you can't always avoid doing harm. If you're falling, you have to break your fall somehow, either with your hand or your head. If you're sick, you either suffer the pain of an operation or face the prospect of ill health and maybe death. Morally, you can't make everything perfect by your actions. But isn't it contradictory for you to say I'm obliged to choose evil?

When we talk about what we should do, we're talking about things that necessarily are good to do; otherwise, how could we be obligated to do them. So how can you say that we should do what we know is evil? This is the same as saying that it's good to do evil — an obvious contradiction in terms.

In some situations, any choice is unfortunate. If our country is attacked, it's better to choose a defense that loses 1,000 soldiers rather than one that loses 10,000. But we don't choose that the 1,000 should die, nor do we kill them: the enemy does that. Rather, we permit the evil that the enemy does because any other choice would let the enemy do greater evil.

However, when you choose to kill one innocent person to save a hundred others, it's a different story. You may not want anyone to die, but you are, in fact, the one who actually kills the innocent person. You're not merely permitting this evil; you're choosing it. But choosing to do evil is not permissible; and it can't be obligatory, not even to avoid a greater evil.

You may have to permit a lesser evil so that a greater one can be prevented. But you must never choose a lesser evil, and you must always refuse to do evil yourself.

The only practical knowledge all men have naturally in common is that we must do good and avoid evil.
Jacques Maritain
Rights of Man and Natural Law, II

Competition
breeds success

If you want the best of something, let people compete for it. That's how we get better. That's how discoveries are made. That's how innovation is encouraged.

Consider how competition spurs on personal initiative. The reason that the U.S. National Soccer Team did so much better at this year's World Cup is that the competition in college soccer and Major League Soccer has recently become so much better. When you have to really work for your place on the roster, everyone gets better, and it benefits the entire team.

Look at our economy. We owe our prosperity to the free market, in which people vie with each other to see who can provide the best goods and services. We've seen what lack of competition does: look at the collapse of the Soviet Union. They just couldn't keep up with our economy. It's competition that has got us here, and only competition can keep us on top.

Competition is good. Without it, we'll never find out what we can really do. Competition brings out what's best in us. *Competition breeds success.*

Good management can never be universally established but in consequence of that free and universal competition which forces everyone to have recourse to it for self-defence.
Adam Smith
Wealth of Nations, I, 10

I T'S TRUE THAT competition pushes people to try their hardest. If the only way you can be successful is to do better than someone else, you have to work to your full potential. This almost always results in improvement — in sports, academics, business, and other endeavors. But can pitting people against each other ever be the basis for successful friendships and communities?

If the ideal is to get ahead of the other guy, aren't we inviting envy and resentment? We'll hope the other guy fails so that we'll get ahead. And we'll resent the fact that someone else is chosen instead of us. Is this a recipe for cooperation? Can teams, families, or businesses thrive under such a model?

Of course, if we compete in being morally good, we've solved the problem. If I try to be kinder and more generous than you, and you try to be kinder and more generous than I, it seems that that we're bound to be successful as friends. And although we might be envious at other people being better than we, if we're committed to being good, we'll strive to overcome this envy.

The original meaning of "competition" is actually rather close to this competition in moral virtue. To compete literally means "to ask or seek together." Given this root understanding of competition, it is clearly a good thing to compete in every aspect of life. To compete in sports, business, or virtue means agreeing to work hard for the benefit of all. This is surely a good.

Understood as the striving to get ahead, competition tends to breed economic and athletic success. But understood as working hard together, competition is success.

Competition, founded upon the conflicting interests of individuals, is in reality far less productive of wealth and enterprise than cooperation.
Robert Hugh Benson
A City Set on a Hill

Don't believe
a thing he says

Why should I even bother to reply?
His argument is so predictable. It's
just what you'd expect him to say.
I can't even stand to listen to him.

You can't expect any truth out of him. After all, look at the
people around him. Anybody in that group is far gone. They're
so close-minded. It's obvious that they've got their minds made
up and won't listen to reason. It's really hopeless. I wouldn't
give him the time of day. The ideas of those kinds of people
are worthless at best, and even a threat to the common good.

Not only does he have questionable associates; his background and track record are suspect, too. He's not educated.
You can't expect the truth from someone who hasn't even been
to college. His personal life hasn't exactly been stellar, either.
You shouldn't take advice from someone who leads an immoral
life like he does. Don't waste your time listening to him.

Really. It's hard to comprehend how anyone
could take someone like him seriously. That
kind of person's ideas just can't be right.
Don't believe a thing he says.

*It is a strong presumption against all super-
natural relations that they are observed chiefly to
abound among ignorant and barbarous nations.*
David Hume
On Miracles

I T'S TRUE THAT the arguments of some people merely parrot some party line. They can be narrow-minded and bigoted. We also have to be careful about accepting the opinions of people leading chaotic or immoral lives. It's unlikely that they'll give the best advice. But when you dismiss someone's argument because of who he is, aren't you being a bigot, too?

You wouldn't want someone to judge your ideas merely in terms of your associations and your background, would you? Shouldn't we judge arguments on their merits instead of according to who presents them? Shouldn't we look for consistency and truth rather than apply a political or personal litmus test?

We all belong to groups to whom we feel bonds of loyalty. And we tend to reject the positions of our group's perceived enemies. But it's irrational to declare an argument false simply because we don't like who's presenting it. We must look at the evidence and not let our imaginations, emotions, or prejudices prevent us from thinking clearly and judging fairly.

Otherwise, we're headed down the road to prejudice and injustice without end. Isn't racism based precisely on this judging people by personal preference rather than objective evidence? Think of the dangers of ethnic profiling and religious persecution. Only if we insist on judging arguments in terms of truth and justice, can we avoid these dangers.

> *Don't believe anything he says just because he says it, but don't reject anything he says just because he says it, either. Believe what he says if it's true; reject it if it's false.*

Do not consider who the person is you are listening to, but whatever good he says commit to memory.
St. Thomas Aquinas
"Letter to Brother John on How to Study"

Don't bite off more than you can chew

Watch what you do. Don't try to tackle something that's too much for you. If you're going to be successful, you have to stay within your comfort zone.

When you take too big a bite of food, you have to spit it out or choke — so it is with life. If you take on more than you're ready for, you'll either have to give it up or get hurt. If you have to give it up, it's a waste of time and resources. In school, it's not worth taking an advanced math course before you're ready for it. You'll just be frustrated and have to go back anyway.

Besides this waste of time and resources, your taking on more than you can handle can really hurt you. Too much physical work may injure your body. If your task is intellectual or moral, trying to do too much may cause permanent psychological or moral damage. You'll end up losing confidence in yourself, or you'll be forced to compromise your moral principles.

So don't be overzealous in your pursuits.
It'll only lead you to disaster. Choose
only goals that you know are doable.
Don't bite off more than you can chew.

For any man who hath a house to found,
Runs not at once the labor to begin
With reckless hand, but first will look around,
And send his heart's line outward from within,
To see how best of all his end to win.
Geoffrey Chaucer
Troilus and Cressida

I T'S TRUE THAT trying to accomplish something beyond your means is a dangerous enterprise. You may either have to give up the project or suffer harm under its crushing load. It's prudent to keep your sights on what you have a reasonable chance of accomplishing. But can you ever make any real strides if you never step out beyond what's easy and safe?

Think of those who have made breakthroughs in science. If they had stayed in their comfort zones, they never would have gone beyond the current scientific knowledge. And think about the great explorers. They had to take on the unknown and the fearful to break out of their own worlds to discover new ones.

Most of us won't make dramatic breakthroughs in science or exploration, but we all need to reach beyond ourselves to be successful. The only way to get better is to take on more than you're certain you can handle. This is true of sports: you'll never know how good you can be unless you push your limits. It's also true of the arts and academic pursuits in general.

Even more important is the need to go beyond yourself in human relations. No one is always easy to understand or to live with. Friendships only grow because each person does more for the other than what comes easily. The only way for us to strengthen our communities is to reach out to one another. We have to go above and beyond what we may feel is our share.

If you bite off too much, you may hurt yourself physically, mentally, or even morally; but if you don't take big bites, you'll never know what good you can do.

That which we are, we are;
One equal-temper of heroic hearts,
Made weak by time and fate,
But strong in will/To strive, to seek,
To find, and not to yield.
Alfred Lord Tennyson
"Ulysses"

Don't cast pearls before swine

Why give people things they can't or won't appreciate? Why try to tell them what they can't or won't understand? You're just wasting time and resources.

You've got to know your audience. You can't expect young teenagers to appreciate the piano sonatas of Bach or the art treasures of the Louvre Museum. They don't care about such things, so you're bound to fail. There's no point in trying to teach a ten-year-old the intricacies of nuclear physics or the subtleties of psychology; she couldn't make sense of them.

Not only is it a waste of time to give people what they can't appreciate or understand; it may cause them harm. By trying to force culture on them, you'll just deepen their dislike for such things. By trying to teach people too much, you're likely to confuse them, undermining their confidence in reason. And if they don't want to learn, they'll grow to hate reason.

Don't bother trying to give good things to those who can't or won't accept them. If you do, they'll either ignore or reject them. *Don't cast pearls before swine.*

Do not give to dogs what is holy; and do not throw your pearls before swine, lest they trample them under foot and turn and attack you.
St. Matthew
Gospel of *Matthew* 7:6

I T'S TRUE THAT we should always try to tailor what we give people to what they're able to understand and accept. After all, the purpose of giving is to benefit the recipients. If they're not benefiting from our gifts or teaching, then our efforts are in vain, and may even harm those we hope to help. But how do you know who can't or won't benefit from your gifts?

What if you misjudge someone's capacity or motivation? You may deprive her of something truly good and useful because you don't think she'll appreciate or understand it. There's a danger of pride and injustice here. We should never sell short the abilities or willingness of our fellow human beings.

People can feel threatened by the truth. When they hear it, they grow more entrenched against it. You should do everything you can to make truth and virtue attractive. But anybody can close his mind to truth or his heart to love. You're not responsible for other people's perversity of will: they are. You're responsible for being as honest and generous as you can be.

Sure, in many cases it seems unlikely that people will care about what you have to share; they may not even want to listen. But that's no reason to give up trying to help them appreciate what is beautiful, know what is true, and do what is good. Better to risk aiming too high and being rejected than aiming too low just to avoid the embarrassment and disappointment of rejection.

> *Casting pearls before swine is a waste of riches, for they can't appreciate beauty or understand truth and virtue. But don't be too quick to cast your fellow human beings as swine.*

To all who desire in humbleness to learn, I offer freely the gifts that God, who gives abundantly and undemandingly to all, has deigned to grant freely to me.
Theophilus
On Divers Arts, Prologue to the First Book

Don't let school get in the way of your education

Life's real lessons are never learned in classrooms. School is nothing but rote learning. You memorize what teachers think is important and spit it back at them.

People say you only get out of school what you put in. But it's not true. What difference does it make how hard I try when what they're telling me is irrelevant? Why should I pay attention to teachers droning on about stuff that bores them and bores me? No learning takes place in class. If I learn anything, it's not because of school but in spite of it.

The only way to get to know what's really true and good is to take a hands-on approach. Then you can remember what you learn. It's what you do with your friends and free time that matters, not what's found in books and the classroom. Instead of spending your time trapped in some ivory tower, find out how real people live.

Don't be fooled. You'll never find out what life's about by studying. Life's too short. *Don't let school get in the way of your education.*

We receive three educations, one from our parents, one from our teachers, and one from the world. The third contradicts the first two.
Montesquieu
Spirit of Laws, Bk. 4

I T'S TRUE THAT there's much more to education than can be found in school. You can discover a lot on your own. You learn about the environment by getting out in it. You discover the past through movies that bring it to life. To understand human relations, you have to get involved with people. But by rejecting school, do you stand in the way of your education?

Aren't there resources in school that you'd have a hard time matching elsewhere? No doubt, not every course excites you, and not every teacher is inspiring. But especially in high school and college, isn't there a wealth of information and expertise there for the taking by the interested student?

Think of the help that books and a well-ordered curriculum offer. They're a repository of the discoveries and insights of generations of intelligent, dedicated human beings. Without books and curriculum, you'd have to discover everything on your own. With them, you can focus on contributing some new and distinctive feature to the collective wisdom of the world.

But schools offer an even more valuable resource: teachers. Teachers are living repositories of learning. Of course, not every teacher is equally brilliant or a master of his or her field. But most have a real love for what they teach, and nothing pleases them more than to help interested students. Don't see school as just the structure: try to find the life within the structure.

> *School is definitely not the only place to get an education, but your refusal to take advantage of its resources can stand in the way of your education.*

I still prefer the daylight of a good school to the dark solitude of a private education.
Quintilian
Institutio Oratoria, I, 2

The end justifies the means

Everybody justifies the means by the end. Indeed, the only possible reason for choosing a particular means to get somewhere is so you can get there.

We're always justifying bad means by good ends. Parents punish their children so they'll be good. Students study hard to get good grades. We accept pain if it gets us the things that we want. We sweat and strain in practice to win games. We choose painful surgery because we'll be better off in the end. No one chooses pain for its own sake. The end justifies it.

The same thing's true of moral decisions. Sometimes we have to do bad things in order to accomplish some greater good. Parents lie to their children to protect them from dangers. Sometimes a coach is unfair to one player in order to do what's best for the whole team. Governments often have to sacrifice the rights of a minority for the good of the majority.

Face it! Sometimes you have to do a little evil if you want to make things better. As long as the end result is good, it doesn't matter how you get there. *The end justifies the means.*

With respect to goodness and badness, as it is with everything else that is not itself either pleasure or pain, so it is with motives. Motives are good or bad only on account of their effects.
Jeremy Bentham
Principles of Morals and Legislation, Ch. 4

I T'S TRUE THAT we consider the end to be more important than the means. We only choose the means because of the end. And we rightly think that a good end, such as health, can justify surgery or tiring exercise, even though these are painful. But if a means is morally evil, can we choose it without violating the most basic principle of morality: don't do evil?

No one thinks that we should intentionally choose an evil end. When we act, the purpose we have in mind should be good. But nobody does anything without some good end in mind — such as pleasure, power, or success. Even the 9/11 terrorists thought it good to strike a blow against American capitalism.

But every chosen means is also an end; that is, it's something we freely intend to do. So it, too, should be good, or at least morally neutral, like pain. No one enjoys pain, but without it we couldn't survive. Pain helps us avoid what's harmful to us. But moral evil is clearly different from pain. Most obviously, moral evil deserves to be punished whereas pain does not.

For an act to be good, all its parts must be good. Both my ultimate goal, and the way I reach that goal must be good. Although the goal of saving ten hostages is certainly noble, achieving this goal by choosing to kill an innocent person isn't permissible, since killing innocent people is clearly wrong. Never do evil so that good may come. It doesn't make sense.

A good end sometimes justifies a painful means. But since we should never intentionally choose moral evil, a good end never justifies a morally evil means.

Whether the majority agree or not, and whether we must still suffer worse things than we do now, one must never do wrong. Nor must one, when wronged inflict wrong in return.
Plato
Crito, 49b

Everyone else does it

Why can't I do it? Everyone's doing it. You say it's wrong, but nobody agrees with you. What are the chances that you're right and everybody else is wrong?

If everyone's doing it, then it's either natural or everyone agrees that it's good (which comes to the same thing). Everyone downloads music from the internet for free. Everyone has cheated on homework or quizzes at one time or another. Everyone drives too fast when cops aren't around. It's unnatural to be honest and law-abiding all the time. Nobody lives that way.

Right and wrong are simply what most people do. We're all free to decide how we want to live. There are no laws that are written in stone. In a democracy, the people have the power and authority to make the laws. So laws reflect their opinions. Social convention works the same way. What all or most people do becomes the rule. There's no other standard.

Right and wrong can't be defined apart from current behavior. It's all a matter of majority opinion, anyway. So why won't you let me do it? *Everyone else does it.*

Modern morality consists in accepting the standards of one's own age.
Oscar Wilde
The Picture of Dorian Gray, Ch. 6

I T'S TRUE THAT cultures or generations develop certain ways of doing things that become part of their identities. There's nothing wrong with this so long as these activities are not immoral. Human beings need to belong to groups. We're social animals and enjoy doing things together. But are right and wrong established by percentages and trends?

Many customs and popular trends need no justification. You don't need an elaborate defense for following fashions in clothing. The crowd's growing enthusiasm for a sports team or popular musician is reason enough to like them. But if there is some moral seriousness to your activity, it's a different story.

Mere reference to the percentage of people who believe something or who do something is a poor way to gauge its truth or goodness. No one would say we ought to judge the truth of scientific theories by what most people think. Nor should we legislate justice based on simple majorities. If we did, there'd be nothing to keep us from treating minorities unjustly.

And if trends dictate morality, we face the odd conclusion that the more that people do what's wrong, the less wrong it gets. If the percentage of people who steal increases from 40% to 80%, stealing becomes half as bad. If murder rates triple, murder becomes only one third as wrong. In other words, as things get worse, they're really getting better. But this is absurd.

What everyone else does may be a safe guide for fashion, but not for morality. There can be a morally good community only when we do what's just and everyone else does it, too.

Nor is the people's judgment always true:
The most may err as grossly as the few.
John Dryden
"Absalom and Achitophel"

Everyone's got a right to his own opinion

I've got a right to believe anything I want. So do you; so does everyone. No one can say what the truth is for certain. We all have to make up our own minds.

Nobody has a monopoly on truth. Everyone should be heard. This is how progress is made. It's a joint effort. No one should feel threatened by what comes to light. If we all voice our opinions, the chances are good that we'll see things from all angles. This is the way scientific advances are made. Many different opinions contribute to our knowledge of the truth.

Nor does anyone have a monopoly on virtue. It's not just the educated or the religious who are good. Everyone's good in some way. There are lots of ways to be good, lots of worth-while causes to support. Some people give money to charity. Others fight for the environment or animal rights. Some think it's better just to take care of yourself and stay out of trouble.

The fact is, people don't agree about what's really true and good. I don't care what the experts say. *Everyone's got a right to his own opinion.*

Every man has a right to utter what he thinks is truth, and every other man has a right to knock him down for it.
Samuel Johnson
in Boswell's *Life of Johnson*

I T'S TRUE THAT people should be free to voice their opinions. It's essential for cooperative learning. Nobody knows everything; there's much we can learn from one another. To force everyone to have the same opinion would shut down human intelligence. But does the fact that everyone has a right to his own opinion mean that everyone's opinion is equally right?

Say, for example, that my opinion is that nobody else has a right to an opinion. Is this as acceptable to you as your opinion that everyone has a right to an opinion? Obviously not. In order to accept my opinion, you'd have to give up your own. If opinions contradict each other, they can't both be true or right.

If we don't object to conflicting opinions, it's only because we don't care about their truth. It's when people press to have their opinions accepted as true that we run into trouble. At that point, we have to determine which opinion is true. Otherwise we'll just have animosity. Both sides must commit themselves to accepting the opinion backed by the best evidence.

Given the difficulty of sorting true from false opinions, we might be inclined to dodge the issue by breaking off the conversation. But this won't do. Although everyone has the right to his own opinion, everyone's also responsible for trying to turn their opinions into truth. If we sidestep this duty, we invite ignorance and injustice into our lives and communities.

> *It's essential for living and learning in a community that everyone should be heard. But, although everyone has a right to his own opinion, not everyone's opinion is right.*

Admitting that everyone's opinion is true, Protagoras must admit the truth of his opponent's belief about his own belief. That is, he must admit that his own belief is false.
Plato
Theaetetus, 171a

Everything's determined by the laws of physics

All the different things in the world have one thing in common. They obey the laws of physics. Ultimately, these laws determine everything.

Physics tells us that there are four fundamental forces at work in the universe: gravity, electromagnetism, the strong force, and the weak force. The first two affect interrelations among things at the atomic level and above; the second two forces are found within the atom itself. All material things are subject to these forces. They are the root causes of everything in the universe.

Even living things are subject to these forces. We're used to thinking of living things as essentially different from rocks, but the same physical forces operate in rocks, trees, dogs, and us. Biology is just a matter of chemistry, chemistry a matter of physics. As the most basic of all explanations, physics has the ability, at least in theory, to explain everything.

Everything has a cause. If we analyze the world, we find that it can all be explained in terms of fundamental physical causes. Ultimately, *every-thing's determined by the laws of physics.*

There is absolute determinism in all the sciences because every phenomenon is necessarily linked with physico-chemical conditions. I mean to prove that it is the same with living bodies, and that for them also determinism exists.
Claude Bernard
Experimental Medicine, II, 1

I T'S TRUE THAT physics has progressed to the point of identifying four fundamental forces that are root causes of all interactions among physical things, from stars to subatomic particles. And since living things are also material, these physical laws hold for them, as well. But if everything's determined by physical forces, why do you try to get me to agree with you?

If thinking is really just matter in motion, can you and I even understand each other? After all, matter can't be in two places at once. When you and I think of what "elephant" means, the matter and motion in your brain are not the same as in my brain. So, on your model of reality, we literally can't think the same thing.

And why try to convince me with your arguments? How can I choose to agree with you even if you're right? All you can expect from me is mindless conformity or arbitrary thoughts, caused, not by your arguments, but by matter in motion. This is not agreement or disagreement, for it's a product of physical force, not meaningful evidence. Why do you waste your time?

If thought is determined solely by physical forces, we can't know it — or know anything at all. But if you see that this is so, then you've shown that at least one thing — your thought — is not controlled by these forces. If you insist on making up your own mind on the matter and trying to convince me, then that's another thing undetermined by physics — your free choice.

If everything's determined by physics, we can't know it, nor choose to share this knowledge. So we can determine this much: physics alone can't explain knowledge and choice.

If my mental processes are wholly determined by the motions of atoms in my brain, I have no reason to suppose they're true . . . and hence I have no reason for supposing my brain to be composed of atoms.
J. B. S. Haldane
Possible Worlds

Experience is the best teacher

There's no school like the school of hard knocks. Read all the books you like, but if you want to learn about the real world, you've got to experience it.

What good does it do to repeat what other people have said and done? You end up like some programmed computer. To learn, you have to ask questions, but all school does is shove answers down your throat. All this advice from dead historians and philosophers is irrelevant to living in the modern world. If you want to know what's important, get out and live.

To know, you have to do. Sure, in the beginning, you'll make mistakes, but that's how you learn. You learn to handle money by overspending. The same thing's true of morality. You learn what not to do by getting punished when you're caught doing it. You learn not to hurt others by seeing them suffer and by experiencing the pain of feeling guilty about hurting them.

Whether it's money management or morality, you don't really learn anything until you've gone through it yourself. Trust me: *experience is the best teacher.*

That which we perform by art after learning, we first learn by performing. We become builders by building and lyre-players by playing the lyre. And we become just by doing what is just, temperate by doing what is temperate, and brave by doing brave deeds.
Aristotle
Nicomachean Ethics, II, 1

I'T'S TRUE THAT there are many things we can only learn through experience. We can't learn to play a sport or musical instrument without the experience of practice. We can't grow in courage or self-control without experiencing challenges and overcoming them by doing what's right. But if experience really is the best teacher, why should I listen to you?

In fact, if experience is the best teacher, why should I bother to read books or accept anybody's word as authoritative? But imagine the time and difficulty involved in learning everything from scratch. How could we make any progress in the sciences or know anything of the past? Books are a great help here.

And what about moral learning? Do we need the experience of doing something wrong to know it's wrong? If so, then the best way to learn that rape and murder are wrong is to rape and murder. But no one believes this. Not only is it false that you've got to experience an action to know it's wrong; doing wrong things actually corrupts our moral knowledge.

The more we experience doing wrong, the less wrong it begins to seem. If we cheat or lie once, our conscience bothers us. If we lie or cheat again, and again, we soon lose our sense of how wrong it is. We grow accustomed to lying or cheating, and they begin to seem normal. The experience of doing wrong leads to worse judgments, not better ones.

*Where practice makes perfect, experience
is the best teacher. But where practice makes
you imperfect — as in immoral actions —
experience is the worst of teachers.*

*All our historical beliefs, most of our geographical
beliefs, many of the beliefs about matters that
concern us in daily life, are accepted on the
authority of other human beings.*
C. S. Lewis
"On Obstinacy in Belief"

Familiarity breeds contempt

I'm tired of the local scene. Nothing new or exciting ever happens to me. How could anyone be inspired by these surroundings? I need a change of place.

My family and friends are so predictable. I hear the same dull platitudes from my Dad; Mom nags me all the time about doing my part for the family. My high school has got to be the most pathetic and useless school in the whole country. Our town can't afford to build a school with decent facilities or hire good teachers. The education here is a waste of time.

Worse: my boring family and community are holding me back. If only my parents were more with it, I could do lots of exciting things, like traveling to exotic places or finding an unusual job in some lively city far from here. And if I lived in another town with better schools, I'd surely be able to get into a really good college. Then I could be a success and find happiness.

I hate my life. I'm trapped by my family and school. How can I be expected to survive among such dull people, never mind fulfilling my potential? *Familiarity breeds contempt.*

It is a sign of our defectiveness that acquaintance and familiarity disgust us with one another.
Michel de Montaigne
Apology for Raymond Sebond

I T'S TRUE THAT what's familiar can become routine and leave us bored and oppressed. What we're used to seems to offer nothing new. We need to be stimulated by exciting people and events. We can even begin to resent the limitations of the places and people around us. But without familiarity, can you ever break through to new levels of creativity and success?

Think about the games you play and your friendships. How can you advance to new and exciting levels of a video game unless you're familiar with the machine and the program? Can your joy in sports grow if you don't master the rules and skills involved? Do friendships deepen without familiarity?

In these areas at least, far from leading to contempt, familiarity brings advanced appreciation and enjoyment. Math is more fun when you get better at it, and this requires familiarity. The delight and excitement of playing music increases as you get better at playing your instrument. Familiarity with a hockey stick or a softball bat is essential for progress in these sports.

Familiarity is most valuable in human relations. Close friends don't have to set up barriers of formality or playfulness. Their intimacy frees them to develop their talents and generosity. In fact, contempt for people often comes from lack of familiarity, which can cause harmful prejudices. Familiarity removes this contempt. With familiarity comes trust and respect.

Familiarity that's just routine breeds contempt.
But only through familiarity can we grow in
skill and understanding. Familiarity can and
should breed appreciation and progress.

Friendship requires time and familiarity; men can't
accept each other and be friends till each has shown
himself dear and trustworthy to the other.
Aristotle
Nicomachean Ethics, IX, 4

Foolish consistency is the hobgoblin of little minds

Don't get stuck in a rut. Take chances. Branch out. Who cares if you contradict yourself? The ability and the courage to change your mind are signs of life.

Life's not a mathematical equation. Stuff happens. You get new information; the world around you changes; you come to see things from a different perspective. When this happens, it only makes sense to change your mind. New problems call for new solutions. It's the way of scientific progress — new discoveries force us to abandon what we thought was true.

And it's also the way of moral progress. It's easy to follow the rules. But life isn't just black and white. You've got to be willing to contradict yourself in order to do what's best. You certainly don't want to be bound by what you've done up to now if you realize that it's been wrong. You've got to be flexible enough to handle the unique challenges of life.

You've got to be ready for anything. Who knows what challenges you'll meet tomorrow? Don't bind yourself with silly rules. *Foolish consistency is the hobgoblin of little minds.*

A foolish consistency is the hobgoblin of little minds,
adored by little statesmen and philosophers and divines.
With consistency a great soul has simply nothing to do.
Ralph Waldo Emerson
"Self-Reliance"

I T'S TRUE THAT consistency that will not consider other options is narrow-minded and restrictive. If we bind ourselves to fixed ideas, we may miss out on new and better ways of understanding the world. If we're bound to certain habits, we may close ourselves off from what's really important. But can the narrow minds you deplore expand without consistency?

Isn't it because new evidence isn't consistent with our old way of thinking that we change? We don't want our understanding to be inconsistent with how things really are. Isn't this how scientific progress works? We don't settle for inconsistency; we seek theories that are consistent with the evidence.

In fact, all expansion of minds requires consistency. You can't advance in your knowledge of geometry without following the rules and axioms. You can't learn more about the ways of the speckled grouse without meshing your observations with the knowledge you have. If you want to make any argument for anything, you have to be consistent in your language and logic.

As for moral progress, it too requires consistency. Why should we be open to new ways of doing things unless it's a moral rule that people ought to be open? How could we ever know that an act such as killing is wrong unless we see that it violates some moral standard? But rules and standards are forms of consistency. All meaningful moral progress requires them.

Foolish consistency does interfere with intellectual and moral growth. But wise consistency in principles and efforts keeps us from growing more foolish.

Our children are counting on us for two things: consistency and structure. Children need parents who say what they mean, mean what they say, and do what they say they are going to do.
Barbara Coloroso
Kids Are Worth It, Ch. 6

A friend in need is a friend indeed

You find out who your friends are when you're in trouble. Those who just say they're your friends walk away. Your real friends are there to help and comfort you.

Real friends are interested in who you are, not what you have. Plenty of people will come around if you're rich or famous. But they're not real friends. If you lose your money or your fame, they're gone. They're fair-weather friends, friends in greed, but not in need. True friends don't care about externals. They love you for your own sake, not for what you can do for them.

Desperate straits bring out your best friends. They're the ones who stand by you through a long illness, or a major loss. They're always there to comfort you, to grieve with you, and to be part of the healing process. They're patient and persevering. They refuse to give up on you, even at those times when you give up on yourself. Such friends are few, but they're invaluable.

It's a real friend who helps you when you can't give anything back, who sacrifices time and pleasure for your happiness. *A friend in need is a friend indeed.*

Real friendship is shown in times of trouble; prosperity is full of friends.
Euripides
Hecuba, 251

I T'S TRUE THAT friends help you when you're in need. And you can tell who your real friends are because they'll stick by you through thick and thin. They're not interested in you because of what you do for them, but because you're you. Such selfless friends are helpful to you in many ways and are precious, indeed. But is friendship based on need really friendship?

Certainly, friends care about each other's needs. But if friendship were based primarily on needs, it would end when the needs ended. But that's not really friendship. Friendship is between two or more people; if ours is based solely on what you do for me, then it's really not about us — it's about me.

If friendship is a unity of persons, then it must have at its center something that can be shared. But my need and your need or my pleasure and your pleasure can't really be shared. They're particular to one of us. Real friendship is based on some common good that we pursue together. It could be a hobby or a sport. It could be a love of museums or of the outdoors.

The best of such goods are things like truth, virtue, and love. Not only can these things be shared, but they also increase when they're shared. The more I have of them, the more you can have them, too. They keep on growing, and so does the friendship based on them. To want these things for your friend, is to care about your friend's good, not your own needs.

A friend in need is certainly a friend. But those who do more than satisfy needs by striving to help each other be wise and good are true friends in heart, in mind, and in deed.

Since friendship depends more on loving than on being loved, loving seems to be the virtue of a friend.
Aristotle
Nicomachean Ethics, VIII, 10

Have the courage
of your convictions

You've got to live by your principles.
When you know you're right, don't back
down just because somebody disagrees
with you. Stand by what you believe.

Think of the teacher who asks a question in math class.
You give your answer, and she says, "Are you sure?" If you're
sure of your response, say, "Yes." Don't fall for her rhetorical
trick and hedge your bet. We all know that if you change
your answer for this reason, you're likely to be wrong.
The same is true for other questions you face in life.

It can be hard to find out what's really true and good. You
have to understand facts and evaluate evidence. But once you
know that something's true or good, don't change your mind
until you meet evidence stronger than what you've already
seen. This takes courage because many people, whether
sincerely or with an ax to grind, will challenge you.

Don't let fear or pressure from others make you
back down from what you know is true. Only
a better argument should change your mind.
Have the courage of your convictions.

*Some of us were ambivalent, but we didn't do
ambivalence well in America. We do courage
of convictions. We do might makes right.
Ambivalence is French. Certainty is American.*
Anna Quindlen
Thinking Out Loud

I T'S TRUE THAT you have to stand up for what you think is true and good. You shouldn't give up your convictions for the sake of convenience or from fear of ridicule. There's always somebody who disagrees with you. It takes courage to endure being challenged or disliked. But when you defend your convictions, is this standing up for what's right, or for yourself?

Do you want things the right way or your way? Is your conviction based on evidence, or just on what you wish to be true? We can be convinced of something for all sorts of reasons besides evidence: its emotional appeal, the fact that someone we like believes it, or just our stubbornness.

But the fact that we find an idea appealing doesn't justify our defending it. I may like to feel I'm the best, but that doesn't mean I am. Nor are opinions justified because of who holds them. The fact that someone is successful, rich, or famous doesn't prove that that person knows what's true or right. Even so-called "experts" in the field may be misleading or wrong.

Even if your conviction is based on some evidence and rational argument, you still have to guard against defending the conviction primarily because it's your conviction. If you don't, you may reject evidence that counts against your position. When this happens, the basis of your defense shifts quickly from rational conviction to pride or stubbornness.

> *It's good to have the courage of your convictions, but when evidence suggests you may be wrong, you need to have the courage to reexamine and even reject them.*

We must bring the courage of our minds covetous of truth, and truth only, prepared to hear all things, and decide all things, according to evidence.
Frances Wright
Course of Popular Lectures, 1

He who hesitates is lost

You've got to strike while the iron is hot. Make the most of your opportunities. If you wait, it may be too late. You may never have the same chance again.

In team sports, when the defense opens up for an instant, you've got to make that pass or shoot. If you don't, the scoring opportunity is past; you may not get another. In finance, when the market is just beginning to expand, you have to invest. Otherwise, you lose your opportunity to get ahead. And if you don't sell at the right time, you could lose everything.

The same is true in morals. Only by acting promptly in good ways can you build character. It takes courage and boldness to stand up to injustice. Quick action is necessary to defend the common good. If you don't correct injustice right away, it may grow too big to be defeated. You'll miss the chance to help others. Act now while you can still make a difference.

Don't spend so much time contemplating what you should do. By the time you reach a decision, the opportunity may have passed. *He who hesitates is lost.*

While we're talking, envious time is fleeing:
seize the day, put no trust in the future.
Horace
Odes, Bk. 1

IT'S TRUE THAT we shouldn't squander opportunities. There are times when we need to act quickly or we miss the chance to benefit ourselves and others. Lack of commitment confounds thought and action. We should act promptly when a decision has been reached. But if we don't know where we're going or what we should do, should we plunge ahead anyway?

If you're lost in the woods, the worst thing you can do is to charge blindly ahead. You'll just get more lost. Sit down and think about how you might find your way to safety. You might judge the direction you should take by where the sun is; or if you're in the mountains, you might follow a stream.

Not only should we pause to get our sense of direction, but we also need to sort the real from the apparent opportunities. We're bombarded with get-rich-quick invitations that turn out to be scams. Even opportunities to be kind are not always what they seem. We should reflect on whether our generosity will really be helpful, and whether or not we're being patronizing.

To act when you don't know what to do can be bad for others, and it's always bad for you. Your unreflective act sets a bad example for others to follow, and it may bring about bad consequences. But however it affects others, it always harms you by contributing to forming a character that's impulsive, foolish, and rash rather than patient, wise, and courageous.

When the time is right and the path is clear,
he who hesitates loses an opportunity; but
he who is lost and will not hesitate may
lose himself entirely.

Patience is the attendant of wisdom,
not the handmaid of passion.
St. Augustine
On Patience, Ch. 5

If it ain't broke,
don't fix it

Use your common sense. If something
is working fine, then leave it alone.
Why mess around with a good thing?
You're just asking for trouble.

It's simply a matter of efficiency. If a machine is working
fine, don't waste your time and money trying to make it
work better. You're better off putting your energy into repairing
machines that are about to break down, or perhaps inventing
new machines that will take care of other needs you have. Basic
maintenance is fine, but major changes are money misspent.

It's no different in human affairs. If your relationship with
your friend or spouse is doing fine, don't go probing into
possible disagreements that may lurk below the surface. If you
do, you'll create problems that would never have appeared if
you'd left things alone. The same is true in a community or
organization. If the structure works, don't mess with it.

Carry on. Don't worry about what might
go wrong. Leave future problems for the
future. It's enough to put out the fires
at hand. *If it ain't broke, don't fix it.*

It is well: it works well:
let well alone.
Thomas Love Peacock
Misfortunes of Elphin

I T'S TRUE THAT, generally speaking, fixing what's not broken doesn't make sense. With limited resources, it's better to put time and money into what really needs work. As for relationships, it's natural to prioritize them, attending first to those that are strained or broken. But isn't it possible that, for some things, your waiting may actually cause the breaking?

For example, if you don't keep inspecting your car, you may find that a gradually weakening part finally snaps and the car is ruined. Routine inspection would have discovered this weakness before it became a problem. Being pro-active in your troubleshooting can save you a lot of toil and trouble.

In addition to causing problems, waiting can also prevent solutions and progress. Nothing we make, whether mechanical or interpersonal, is the final word. Breakthroughs don't often come out of thin air. They result from knowing that things could be improved and trying improve them. We should work to make things better, not just to keep them from breaking.

With friendship, in fact, work is necessary just to maintain it. It's dangerous to take for granted someone's good will and fidelity. Trust is a fragile thing. It must be constantly renewed. Friendships never stay the same. They're either getting better or worse. We must keep fixing friendships to counteract the tendency toward mere routine and indifference.

> *There's no sense in fixing things that aren't broken; it's just not efficient. But people are not things. If we don't keep fixing personal relationships, they'll break.*

If you leave a thing alone you leave it to a torrent of change.
G. K. Chesterton
Orthodoxy, Ch. 7

If they say so,
it must be true

You can't prove everything by yourself.
There's too much to know and not enough
time to know it. The trick is to find out
who's in the know and then tune in.

We take things on authority all the time. We have to. If you
want to visit some distant place, you've got to believe the
mapmakers. If you're going to trust your car to get you safely
to your destination, you've got to believe in the engineers
who say it's safe. You can't discuss history without trusting in
some authority. If you challenge one, it's because of another.

In social and political issues, you've got to listen to the experts,
whose talent and intelligence has brought them success and
fame. After all, their fame isn't just an accident. They were
smart enough to recognize their opportunities and act on them.
You've got to respect that. When you can't solve the difficult
questions of life, follow the lead of those who know best.

Come on now. You've been around long
enough to know which side to believe.
Listen to the successful and articulate.
If they say so, it must be true.

*He who does not listen to the words
of his elders will surely suffer soon.*
Chinese Proverb

I T'S TRUE THAT we have to rely on authority in many areas of our lives. We can't travel everywhere. We can't reproduce every scientific experiment or verify all the events recorded in the history books. We can't be up to date on every current issue. We have to trust in the judgments of others. But is anything true or false, or right or wrong, just because someone says so?

Don't we have to have some kind of objective evidence to justify our beliefs? If we don't see why something is true, should we accept it? If we don't know that doing something is morally permitted, should we do it? Don't we, at least, have to have evidence that the authorities we trust are trustworthy?

Just because your friend says you can take a direct flight from Boston to Bismarck doesn't mean that it's true. Just because a Nobel-laureate scientist says that cloning is morally permissible doesn't automatically mean it is. The fact that a famous movie star takes a stand on a political issue doesn't show her stand is the right one. You need evidence before you can decide.

Of course, you can't always have direct evidence; but at least you need a reason to think that an authority is legitimate. Being a friend doesn't make a person an expert on air travel. Scientific expertise isn't moral expertise. Fame doesn't give you special insight into politics. It's expertise in the appropriate area that makes a person a legitimate authority.

If they say so, it might be true, particularly
if they know what they're talking about.
But their saying so doesn't make it true —
only evidence can do this.

Whoever in discussion adduces authority
uses not intellect, but rather memory.
Leonardo da Vinci
Notebooks, Bk. 1

If you can't beat 'em, join 'em

Conquer the competition if you can. But why fight a losing battle? If you can't win, change your allegiance. Snatch victory from defeat — just switch sides.

There are two ways to get ahead: you can either overcome the competition or become the competition. When the going gets tough, the second is the way to guarantee success. This is the way business and politics operate all the time. Corporations merge to preserve their market advantage. If your own political party is out of favor, preserve your power by joining the other.

It's not just good for you; it's good for everyone. Why should we beat up on each other and both lose out? By joining forces we can relieve tensions and promote prosperity. This is the broad path of political compromise. Minority positions get absorbed into a richer majority consensus. This merger preserves the peace and ensures future growth and well-being for all.

It's the way of the world. Power rules. If you don't have the power, you have to get it. You can't afford to stand on principle. *If you can't beat 'em, join 'em.*

Mankind likes to think in terms of extreme opposites. The extremes are all right in theory, but when it comes to practical matters, circumstances compel us to compromise.
John Dewey
Experience and Education

I T'S TRUE THAT sometimes the only way to come out on top is to join the other side. If you're unable to achieve victory on your own terms, you may have to accept other terms. Your very survival could depend on it, and it could prove to be best for you and the community as a whole. But what if the competition you could join is not just tough, but in the wrong?

If you decided to join, wouldn't you be cooperating with evil? Should you ever do this? Perhaps all you're seeking is power and glory. If so, then it really doesn't matter whether you get them from winning or joining. But should you be seeking your power and glory, or the good that you hope to gain or protect?

Sometimes, goodness is best served by joining the other side. If you run a small business, working with the competition may bring mutual benefits. Cooperative research, where resources and talent are pooled, shows the value of joining. In a three-way political race, if a candidate knows she can't win, it makes sense for her to join forces with the candidate she favors.

But if disagreement about fundamental beliefs or values separates you from the competition, then to join them when you can't beat them would be hypocrisy or betrayal. Unless you think your opponents are right, giving up your beliefs and accepting theirs is hypocritical. And if the other side is morally wrong, joining them is a betrayal of moral principle. This can't be good.

If you can't beat them and joining them promotes the good you seek, then by all means join them. But if what they seek is wrong, don't join them in their evil.

We shall fight on the beaches, we shall fight on the landing grounds, we shall fight in the fields and in the streets, we shall fight in the hills; we shall never surrender.
Winston Churchill
at Hansard, 6/4/1940

If you've seen one, you've seen them all

Don't focus on each individual. There's no real difference between grains of sand on a beach. Roses are basically the same, and so are horses, sparrows, and foxes.

Real knowledge is about what's universal, what things have in common. This is obvious for mathematics: 2 and 5 don't refer to particular things; they're universal quantities. But the same is basically true for things in the world. Real differences lie between groups of individuals, not the individuals — between species of plants and animals, not the members of a species.

No one has the time to look at the particularities of every individual thing. We have to classify things; it's how we sort out the world. We do it for people, too. People from similar parts of the world or similar backgrounds are obviously alike. The same is true of people with similar personality traits; when you recognize one, you know what to expect of the rest.

To think is to classify. We naturally see things as groups. Individuals don't really matter in our scientific understanding of the world. *If you've seen one, you've seen them all.*

"The individual" is an idea like other ideas.
Harold Rosenberg
Discovering the Present

I T'S TRUE THAT when you come to understand well one member of a group, you understand much about the other members. There's no need to go into the distinguishing features of each. In fact, there's no time. You'd never come to the end of all the particulars. But if you think that "if you've seen one you've seen them all," have you really seen even one?

If I see a rose as merely an example of a particular kind of plant, I haven't really seen the rose. To classify it and so ignore all the particularities unique to it alone is to miss what's most real about it. Sure, it's a particular kind of rose belonging to one branch of the plant kingdom, but it's so much more.

Knowledge does work through universals, but it's the particular thing that we're trying to understand. We must never forget that the primary realities are the individual things. Plants don't exist: particular roses, blackberry bushes, and pine trees do. Knowledge of the common characteristics of things is real knowledge, but it's incomplete. There's always more to know.

When we're talking about human beings, it's especially important to remember the primacy of the person. It's far too easy to pigeonhole people and ignore them as individuals. He's a good athlete; she's a great dancer; he's not very smart; she's mean. You and I know that we don't want to be so easily put in a box and dismissed. Let's not do it to others.

> *To see one is to see something of them all. But no amount of common traits can express the individual's reality. Don't let your knowledge of them all keep you from seeing each one.*

I have seen Frenchmen, Italians, Russians; but man I have never met.
Joseph de Maistre
Considérations sur la France

Ignorance
is bliss

Knowledge brings grief. Why should you spend your time struggling to learn? Anyway, who wants to know bad news? It only makes you depressed.

It takes time and energy to learn, and it only gets harder as you go along. First it's algebra, then geometry; before you know it, you're lost in calculus. And then try to answer the deep philosophical questions of life: all you get is more questions, which are even harder to answer. What's the use? It's easier to coast. What you don't know, won't hurt you.

And if you learn about all the suffering and injustice in the world, you just feel bad. You can't do anything about them anyway. The more you know, the more you despair over the state of the world. It paralyzes you. You might just as well forget all these problems and get on with your life. At least that way, you might be able to accomplish something good.

Knowledge is no help. In fact, it's a large part of the problem. Forget your cares and everybody else's troubles. Don't worry; be happy. *Ignorance is bliss.*

Nothing is more conducive to peace of mind than not having any opinion at all.
Georg Christoph Lichtenberg
Aphorisms

I T'S TRUE THAT knowledge doesn't always seem so good. Gaining knowledge can be hard work. Once you master the basics of a subject, you move on to more difficult matters. And hearing news about the world's problems is painful. There's so little we can do. But if ignorance is bliss, then why do you bother to teach this truth to those who are ignorant of it?

Why try to convince people that there's no benefit in being convinced? If it's really better not to know, then there's no point in communication. And if it's better to be ignorant than to learn, why should I, or anyone else, consider your position? Shouldn't we prefer to be ignorant of what you think?

Your efforts to explain yourself to others presume that knowledge is better than ignorance. If only others understood you, they'd change their minds and agree with you. And what about your questions — the ones you really care about? Is it blissful to have them unanswered? Do you want to be ignorant of who you are, why you're here, and how best to live?

But perhaps you just mean that ignorance about bad things is bliss. We probably could do without the litany of disasters we see in the news, but surely we want to know about the bad things that affect us. Who wants to be ignorant of a tornado coming our way or of crooks in the neighborhood? Only if we know about them can we protect ourselves or prepare for them.

Ignorance of things we can't do anything about frees us from the pain of useless anxiety. But ignorance of the truths and virtues that we need to live well, is ignorance of bliss.

Here is the evil in ignorance: that he who is neither good nor wise is nonetheless satisfied with himself.
Plato
Symposium, 204A

It could
be worse

It's no use complaining. Things are bad,
but not as bad as all that. Think of all the
other things that could've gone wrong.
Be grateful for the good you have.

Instead of a "C" on your exam, you could have gotten an "F".
Instead of $100, they could have stolen $1,000. Instead of the
flu, you could have lung cancer. And there are always people
worse off than you are. Just think of the hungry, the oppressed,
the unemployed. You're not starving, you have your freedom,
and you have a decent job. There's comfort for you here.

Don't let the problems of the world get you down. When
you read about disasters — floods, famines, earthquakes, and
wars — be grateful they aren't worse. At least not all of India
is flooded and not all of Africa starving. At least the terrible
devastation of WWII was limited. You have to keep this perspective on the world's problems; otherwise, you'll go crazy.

You've got to fight defeatism and take a
positive approach to life. When you
think about yourself or the world,
always remember: *it could be worse.*

*"Blessed be nothing," and "The worse
things are, the better they are," are
proverbs which express the tran-
scendentalism of common life.*
Ralph Waldo Emerson
"Circles"

I T'S TRUE THAT things could always be worse. You could have less money than you have now. You could suffer more pain or depression. The suffering of others and evil in the world could be multiplied. Knowing these facts is some grounds for gratefulness. But by emphasizing that it could be worse, do you risk keeping things from getting better?

If you take comfort in the fact that it could be worse, you may grow indifferent to the problems at hand. And if you don't see these problems as they really are, you'll never know what needs to be done to correct them. Such indifference and ignorance are the enemies of wise and generous moral action.

The problems in the world or in our own lives won't go away because we ignore them. Suffering and moral evil are real, and we must face up to them. The fact that someone only stole $100 when he might have stolen $1,000, doesn't make theft any better. The fact that 20% (rather than 40%) of the people of a nation are hungry doesn't make hunger any more acceptable.

There's nobility in enduring patiently the pain we suffer and the wrongs done to us, but should we ignore the suffering and oppression of others? To say, "Your pain could be greater" or "You could be treated worse" is cold comfort, not to say insult. And in our own evil actions, we must never take comfort in the fact that we could have done something even worse.

*It's always true that things could be worse,
so we really should count our blessings.
But never forget: although it could be
worse, it should be better.*

*All things are better and lovelier for the imper-
fections which have been divinely appointed,
that the law of human life may be Effort,
and the law of human judgment, Mercy.*
John Ruskin
The Stones of Venice, Vol. II, Ch. 6

It doesn't matter what you believe, so long as you're sincere

There's nothing worse than hypocrites and liars. What the world needs is honesty. We can't even begin to make progress unless people are sincere.

Sincerity is the lifeblood of politics. It's less important what your position is than that you're involved. Democracy can only work if people sincerely add to the public debate what they believe to be true. There are good people on both sides of any issue. Because both sides are dedicated to their principles, we come up with a pretty good policy. It's the best we can do.

It's the same thing with religious belief or philosophy of life. What's important is not the content of what you believe, but your commitment. All religions have good people who are sincerely committed to their beliefs. And there are plenty of good people who are sincere atheists. The worst thing is just to be indifferent. You've got to commit yourself.

You can tell the people who really care. They're deeply committed to some cause. In the end, *it doesn't matter what you believe, so long as you're sincere.*

Sincerity is a jewel which is pure and transparent, eternal and inestimable.
Christopher Smart
Jubilate Agno, Fragment B

I'S TRUE THAT sincerity is indispensable. People who don't really believe what they say are either hypocrites or deceivers. If you're not honest with yourself, you can't be honest with others. Without sincerity and commitment, no kind of community is possible. But is your plea for sincerity worthy of belief because you're passionate about it, or because it's true?

Some people passionately believe their favorite sports team is the best and that the team's defeat is an act of injustice. Some people sincerely believe that their family, religion, or ethnic group is better than any other. Their sincerity hardly makes them right. Passionate sincerity alone can't justify beliefs.

When two positions are contradictory, both sides can't be right, even if the people who hold them are sincere. So if you think that sincerity is preferable to insincerity, it must be on some other ground. And this can't be mere opinion or belief, for these vary from person to person. There must be something universally good about sincerity, something that can be known.

And, of course, there is. Sincerity is good because honesty is better than hypocrisy and because telling the truth is better than telling lies. You believe this, not just because you're sincerely and passionately attracted by honesty and truth, but because you understand them to be good. In other words, you see that sincerity is not enough; it really does matter what you believe.

> *Without sincerity no community is possible.*
> *But so long as it doesn't matter what we're*
> *sincere about, our community teeters on*
> *the brink of relativism and anarchy.*

Integrity without knowledge is weak
and useless, and knowledge without
integrity is dangerous and dreadful.
Samuel Johnson
Rasselas

It's all fate

What does it matter what I do?
Everything's governed by fate. We're
no more than puppets in the hands
of God. Free choice is an illusion.

I've heard the arguments for the existence of God. They
seem good to me. But if there is an ultimate cause of everything, then it must have infinite power over things. God must
know everything and determine how everything will be. But if
God knows with certainty everything that is going to happen
and if he is the cause of every activity, how can I act freely?

I suppose I could reject the existence of God, but it seems
to me that there are good reasons to believe in such a being.
What am I to do? I find it kind of depressing. Either there's no
ultimate explanation for the way things are (no God), or if
there is such an explanation, I'm not really free. Either way,
life seems futile to me. It's hard to see why I should care.

Somehow, everything must fit together. It
can't be just a matter of chance. But if God
is ordering everything, then there's no room
for freedom. In the end, *it's all fate.*

*No truth is more certain than this, that all
that happens, be it small or great,
happens with absolute necessity.*
Arthur Schopenhauer
Supplement to *The World as Will and Idea*

IT'S TRUE THAT we can be puzzled about freedom in the face of providence or fate. After all, if God is all-knowing and all-powerful, nothing can happen apart from his will. If God's providence determines our actions, we can't be free. But why do you believe that the activity of God takes away your ability to choose freely? Is it necessary that you do so?

Does the fact that God causes everything to exist mean that everything is determined? This would only be true if everything that exists is determined. But if we want to know whether this is true, we have to study the things themselves. And one of the things we have to study is ourselves.

One thing we know about ourselves is that we can make free choices. We know this because we do it. Think about a choice you make — such as to read this book. You can't really think that your free choice is determined. If you did, you wouldn't call it your choice. To say your choice is caused by another would be to say that your choice is not your choice. That makes no sense.

As for saying that the nature of God means that you can't be free, this is untrue. What we know about God is that God is the cause of everything. By giving things existence, God makes things to be what they are, not what they are not. God makes things that are determined by the laws of physics to be determined; and God makes free things like you and me to be free.

There are no good reasons to think you're determined. In fact, it's impossible to think your choices are really determined by something or someone else. Choose well, for fate allows it.

Our will would not be a will if it were not in our power. And since it is in our power, we are free with respect to it.
St. Augustine
On Free Choice of the Will, Bk. 3, Ch. 3

It's better to journey than to arrive

Some people are so focused on arriving that they don't enjoy the trip. You've got to appreciate the surprises and joys that you'll meet along life's way.

When I travel to San Francisco, I could choose to take a plane and get there fast, but I'd rather take my time and drive so that I can see the country. When I go for a hike, it's the hiking that I savor, not the end-point. Likewise, it's the four years I spent in college that I treasure. The many moments of insight and the great friendships matter far more than the diploma.

So it is for life in general. I care much more about the process than the product. So often the goals I set out for myself turn out to be hollow and empty. I want to experience the rich diversity of places and people the world has to offer. This is what's fun and exciting. The idea of arriving at the contemplation of some abstract truth just sounds boring.

Life's a journey so don't worry about where you're going. Experience matters most — not what you accomplish or where you end up. *It's better to journey than to arrive.*

Not the fruit of experience, but experience itself is the end. To burn always with this hard, gemlike flame, to maintain this ecstasy, is success in life.
Walter Pater
Studies in the History of the Renaissance

I T'S TRUE THAT sometimes a journey is as good or even better than its destination. For traveling or hiking, the main purpose is often the process, not the destination. It's really the excitement of exploration and adventure that we enjoy. So, too, as we travel through life, we savor our experiences often for their own sake. But do we ever act without some purpose in mind?

Would you spend hours practicing the piano if you didn't care about becoming a good piano player? Who would ever take the time to learn a foreign language except for the purpose of using it? Would you even go wandering without a desire to relax, or to see what you can see, or to find adventure?

In the case of traveling, the actual last stop in your journey may not be of ultimate importance, but finding adventure along the way is important. Aimless wandering is not something we seek for its own sake. It's the same with going to college. You might go for many different reasons, but if none of these purposes were fulfilled, you would not count college a success.

In terms of "traveling" through life, the priority of arriving is clear. Finding a true friend is better than seeking one. It's better to understand the truth than to muddle along in error. Becoming virtuous is preferable to an endless series of moral failures. Specific goals often disappoint us, but some ends, like friendship, truth, and virtue are continually rewarding.

> Both journeying and arriving are worthy
> of choice. But no journey was ever begun
> without the hope of arriving at some
> place or state of mind.

The most important object of desire is that for the sake of which something is sought. But all things are sought for the sake of happiness. So happiness alone is the object of man's desires.
Boethius
Consolation of Philosophy, Bk. 3, Ch. 10

It's my life

You don't own me. I'm nobody's slave. You can't tell me how to live or how not to live. I have the right to do whatever I want with my life.

People aren't like things: they can't be owned. Even though I received life from my parents, I'm not really theirs. Sure, when I was too young to take care of myself, they told me what to do. They ordered my life because I couldn't. That made sense. But now that I'm an adult, I'll take charge of my life. I'll decide what to do and when to do it. It's nobody's business but my own.

And just because I live in a community and a nation doesn't mean I have any great responsibilities to them. It's my choice how I'll live. As long as my actions don't hurt other people, I can do anything I please. If I want to make a lot of money, I will. If I want to risk my life doing extreme sports, I will. If I just want to chill out and do nothing, that's O.K., too.

So don't tell me what to do with my life. I'll work hard if I want to, or maybe I'll just hang out. And when I want to end my life, I will. You can't stop me. *It's my life.*

Live all you can; it's a mistake not to. It doesn't so much matter what you do in particular, so long as you have your life. If you haven't had that, what have you had?
Henry James
The Ambassadors, Bk. 5

I T'S TRUE THAT no one owns you. Humans are not property to be bought and sold. Nor are they animals to be trained to be useful. Although mothers give life to their children, they don't own them. Every person is unique and should be brought up to take responsibility for his own life. But if people can't be owned, how can it make any sense to say you own your life?

Do you have a deed for it or a receipt? Did you have a right to your life before you were born? Things can be owned; they can be bought and sold as commodities. But people are not things, which is why slavery is wrong. You can own property, but you're not property to be owned — not even owned by you.

But, you will say, "If my life is not my own, whose is it?" Isn't this a false question? It's not that if you don't own yourself, someone else does. No one owns anybody. Sure, when it comes to making important decisions about how you will live, you're in charge. But for anyone to speak of ownership in human relations is simply inappropriate. Human life is not a commodity.

We need a different model to talk about human relations of authority — perhaps stewardship. The clearest example of stewardship is between a parent and a child. The parent's duty is to care for the child for the child's own good. So, too, we should care for ourselves for our own good. This means not just pleasing ourselves, but promoting our human dignity.

It's your freedom and responsibility to develop your life. But since human beings aren't things to be bought and sold, it's not your life to own but to cherish.

A person cannot be a property and so cannot be a thing which can be owned, for it is impossible to be a person and a thing, the proprietor and the property.
Immanuel Kant
"Duties toward the Body in Respect of Sexual Impulse"

It's not how much you know, but how much you care

Who cares how much you know?
The real question is "Do you care about others?" Knowledge is nothing compared to a tender and understanding heart.

Love is the most important thing. People vary widely in intelligence, and even more widely in how much they actually know. But just because you've been to college or got a Ph.D. doesn't mean you're a good person. The best people are those who reach out to others, who care enough to comfort and encourage those around them. It takes heart, not just mind.

What's more, it's the caring person who is best able to get others to learn. Someone who knows a lot about a sport doesn't always make the best coach. Players are only open to learning if they feel their coach cares about them. The same is true with the best teachers. Their genuine commitment to their students puts the students at ease and makes learning fun for them.

People matter more than information.
Friendship matters more than knowledge.
In education and life, *it's not how much you know, but how much you care.*

Good teaching lies in a willingness to care for what happens in our students, ourselves, and the space between us.
Laurent A. Daloz
Effective Teaching and Mentoring, Ch. 9

IT'S TRUE THAT we think the quality of people is better measured by where their hearts are, than by how much they have in their minds. Those who spend lives caring for others deserve our deep admiration. And it's often the case that the caring person is best able to get others to learn. But if we really don't know what's what, how can we care for others as we should?

Is it possible to care without knowing what's worth caring about? Would we say that the person who cares fanatically about his baseball card collection or his own popularity is a good person? Caring that's admirable must be about things that are really good, and it's knowledge that identifies them.

But knowledge is also necessary to help others attain these goods. Would a coach who loved her players but knew nothing about soccer make a good soccer coach? Would a teacher who treated students with respect but knew nothing about calculus make a good calculus teacher? Real caring isn't a warm fuzzy feeling, but a knowledgeable approach to individual needs.

Even the caring involved in friendship is more than a strong emotional attachment. In fact, that emotional attachment may have to be loosened to give the friend freedom to grow. So too, a good leader can't just sympathize with his constituents; he must know how to go about helping them. In teaching, friendship, or leadership, true caring needs knowledge.

How much you know is never a substitute for how much you care. But how well you can see what's worth caring for, and can help others to see it, depends on how much you know.

You can't teach what you don't know.
Dorothy Rich
Education Week, 9/16/1998

It's O.K. as long as it doesn't hurt anybody

People should be allowed to do whatever
they want. Freedom's the rule. As long as
my free choices don't harm you, I don't
see why I can't just do as I please.

Isn't this the basis for our laws? The Declaration of Independence says that we should all be guaranteed "the right to life,
liberty, and the pursuit of happiness." You and I should be free
to seek our happiness in any way we please, provided that
in doing so we don't destroy someone else's life, liberty,
or pursuit of happiness. This is the law's only constraint.

This is as it should be. Actions are right or wrong depending
on their consequences. We can tell whether an act is good
by seeing whether its effects are good. But who doubts that
happiness is a good consequence? It's what we want most of
all. So if something makes me happy and doesn't have bad
consequences for anybody else, I should be allowed to do it.

We've got to be free to choose how we'll live.
My choices are my business. Your choices are
up to you. If you or I decide to do something,
it's O.K. as long as it doesn't hurt anybody.

*The obvious and simple system of natural liberty estab-
lishes itself of its own accord. Every man, as long as
he does not violate the laws of justice, is left perfectly
free to pursue his own interest his own way.*
Adam Smith
Wealth of Nations, IV, 9

I T'S TRUE THAT people should be free to decide how to live their lives. Such freedom is supported in our nation's founding documents. In our legal system, an action is wrong if it harms another. And certainly a concern for consequences is one of the factors in evaluating moral action. But does the fact that an act doesn't hurt other people mean that no one is hurt?

What if I intend to hurt someone, but fail to do so because of some external intervention? Is my act O.K.? After all, I didn't hurt anybody else. But what about me? What happens to me when I choose to do something I know is wrong? Don't I suffer moral harm? Don't I make myself a worse person?

If I lie, don't I become more dishonest? If I drink too much, don't I become intemperate? There's certainly harm done in such actions — harm to me. And the harm does not depend on the consequences of my actions for other people. They might be harmed by my bad actions; but even if they're not, I am. My bad actions immediately and inevitably harm me.

So morality can't be just about the effects of actions. That way of evaluating actions leaves out what's most essential — intentions. It's wrong to try to kill an innocent person, even if you fail. It's wrong to lie, even if no one gets hurt. The key to evaluating a moral act is the intention, not the results. If the intention is bad, the act is morally wrong.

> It's a good thing if my bad actions don't
> end up hurting other people. However, to
> do intentionally what I know to be wrong
> is never O.K., and it always hurts me.

If we do not follow the directions of the one who has knowledge of good and evil, we shall harm and corrupt that part of ourselves that is improved by just actions and destroyed by unjust actions.
Socrates
In Plato's *Crito,* 47d

It's the intention that counts

It's what you mean to do that matters. You can't know all the facts of a situation. You can't foresee all the consequences. You've just got to do what you think is right.

Think of the child who draws a Valentine to his mother on the living-room wall. Sure, he makes a mess of the wall, which will now have to be repainted, but what a gift for Mom! Or what about the mother who buys her son a shirt in what she thinks is the latest style, only to find out that it's not what he wants. Her heart's in the right place. She means well.

Or think of a more serious matter. Imagine that you catch someone stealing and turn him in. It turns out he's been in trouble before, so he's sent to jail. There he falls in with a bad lot. When he gets out, he robs a bank, killing a guard in the process. If you hadn't turned him in, this might never have happened. Is it your fault? No. Your intention was good.

When we judge people's actions, it's not what happens that's most important, but what they intend. All you can do is try to do your best. *It's the intention that counts.*

The main principle in virtue and in character lies in intention.
Aristotle
Nicomachean Ethics, VIII, 15

I T'S TRUE THAT the heart of moral action is intention. It's only because people are free to choose that it makes any sense to blame or praise them. A stone dislodged by an earthquake is not to blame for rolling down a hill and crushing me. Neither are we responsible for what we don't intend. But does this imply that, as long as I mean well, whatever I do is acceptable?

Don't I also have to consider the possible consequences of my act? Don't I have to think ahead? Of course, I can't foresee all the consequences of my actions. But sometimes, they're pretty obvious. If I try to help you by forcing you to do things my way, it won't work. My good intention is not enough.

We don't expect little kids to think ahead and make prudent decisions. So when a three-year-old draws a Valentine on the wall, we see only the generous intention. But if a ten-year-old did the same thing, we wouldn't be quite so understanding. And if a teenager did it, we'd be positively displeased. As children mature, we expect them to exercise more forethought.

As adults, we're expected to have good intentions, to act on them, and to think about their consequences. Good intentions are essential, but it's not enough just to mean well: we've got to back up our good intentions with actions. And when we act, we should act prudently — thinking ahead in order to minimize the harmful effects of our actions and maximize their benefits.

Without good intentions, no one would even try to do what's good. But it's not only the intention that counts; you've also got to have a prudent concern for the consequences.

A moral act derives its rightness or wrongness, not only from what's intended, but also from its circumstances.
St. Thomas Aquinas
Summa Theologica I-II, 18, 9

Just
be yourself

Self-expression is where it's at. Be your
own person. Don't follow the crowd.
Above all, don't pretend to be someone
you're not. Find out who you really are.

After all, why should you conform to some standard of
behavior handed you by other people? Who are they to tell
you who you are or should be? They don't really know you;
they're not on the inside; it's impossible for them to see
things from your perspective. You have to break free from the
expectations of others and find a way to make yourself real.

Just do what you feel like doing and be who you want to be.
You'll be doing the world a favor. Who wants a world in
which everyone is the same? What a boring place that would
be. There'd be no diversity at all. And how would the world
progress if everyone fit the same mold? Be an individual. The
world needs you, with your unique energy, vision, and hope.

To be all you can be, you've got to
find your center. Don't go chasing
after another person's vision of
success. Be unique. *Just be yourself.*

I have my own stern claims and perfect
circle. It denies the name of duty to
many offices that are called duties.
Ralph Waldo Emerson
Self-Reliance

I T'S TRUE THAT you've got to discover your talents and interests and find out how they can best be developed to enhance your personality. That's good for you and good for the community, too. It's always wrong to pretend to be someone you're not. Hypocrisy only ends up harming others and yourself, too. But is it even possible for you to be a self all by yourself?

Did you make yourself? Were you there before you came to be? Obviously not. Then where did you come from? For starters, the matter in your body has been around since matter came into being. Your genetic material has come to you from your parents and from generations of ancestors before them.

What about your talents and intelligence? To some degree, they, too, come from your forebears. Of course, understanding is not inherited: you do it yourself. And how you use your talents and intelligence is really up to you. Yet it's clear that you didn't give yourself free will or the ability to understand, any more than you gave yourself a body or particular talents.

Beyond your material and spiritual elements, you have also been nurtured and educated by family, friends, and community. You didn't reach the point of self-consciousness without being nurtured a couple of years by your parents. You've been cared for by friends, educated by teachers, and included in a community. All these influences contribute to who you are.

> By all means, be yourself. But remember that much of who you are — your life, your intelligence, your community — has been given to you. So be yourself, and be grateful to others.

Like children, elders are a burden. It takes a person of great heart to see the wisdom elders have to offer, and to serve them out of gratitude for the life they have passed on to us.
Kent Nerburn
Letters to My Son, Ch. 26

Let's just agree to disagree

You have your opinion and I have mine. We're never going to agree. So let's not waste our time fighting. It's better to cut our losses and move on to something else.

When people disagree about morality, politics, or religion, there's just not much we can do about it. We can't force them to agree. As a matter of fact, the more we try to make people change their minds, the less likely it is that we'll succeed. The history of political and religious wars makes this quite clear. Debate is endless and unproductive. What we need is peace.

Besides, why should we all agree about such things? Diversity of opinion is healthy. Although I don't agree with you, I should nonetheless respect your ideas, and you should respect mine. Peace is what we really want most, isn't it, and mutual respect? What matters most is that we find a way to get along. Toleration and compromise: these are the twin pillars of democracy.

So let's face it. We'll never agree about morality, politics, or religion. But there is a way that we can still have peace: *let's just agree to disagree.*

Nothing was ever learned by either side in a dispute.
William Hazlitt
"On the Conversation of Authors"

IT'S TRUE THAT the likelihood of everybody agreeing on morality, politics, and religion is pretty slim. Disagreements on such topics are longstanding. Commitments and loyalties are fierce. To prosper, we need the peace that comes from mutual respect. But can I respect your ideas if I think they're wrong? And how can I know whether they're wrong if we don't discuss them?

You say you want peace, but it seems like you only want a cessation of hostilities. Real peace has to be built on some harmony of vision, not mutual disengagement (which leaves people separated and wary of each other). If we're to find this harmony of vision, you and I have to discuss our ideas openly.

But where do we start? It's at those points where we already agree. A couple of them come immediately to mind. First of all, if we're seeking peace, we agree that we should care about our world and try to make it better. Secondly, if we're to take each other's ideas seriously about how to achieve this peace, we agree in our commitment to finding the truth.

Building on our agreement on these points, we can try to expand the range of our consensus. This process can be slow and painful and will require a good deal of patience, honesty, and consistency. Real differences exist between us. On some of them we may not be able to settle our disagreement. But we've got to try. The alternative isn't peace: it's isolation and suspicion.

We should agree to disagree when it avoids meaningless controversy, but we should never agree that avoiding controversy is better than finding justice and truth.

We shall never have a common peace in Europe till we have a common principle in Europe.
G. K. Chesterton
All Things Considered

Life is what you make it

Don't let other people tell you who you should be. They'll try because they want to justify their own choices. Create your own way of life. Choose who you will be.

Who can say what the best way of life is? Infinite possibilities lie before you. It's up to you to decide which ones you'll make real. Just because lifestyles differ does not mean that one is better than another. Being a lawyer is different from being an artist, but each has its own particular value. It's good to be a doctor, but it's also good to teach or go into business.

Freedom is the greatest gift you have. Don't let it go to waste. Although your genetics, social background, and environment influence your behavior, they don't determine what you'll do or who you'll be. They don't force you to read this book. You can stop and do something else anytime you choose. You have the inborn ability to make free choices. Use it.

Opportunity knocks. You have the freedom and the right to decide what gives meaning to your life. Don't give up on what you want. Do it: *life is what you make it.*

Man is simply nothing else but that which he makes of himself. That is the first principle of existentialism.
Jean-Paul Sartre
Existentialism

I T'S TRUE THAT no one knows precisely what's best for someone else. You really do have to make your own way in the world. Genetics, upbringing, and environment don't determine who you'll be. The future is not fixed; you have free will. However, as good as it is to be free and optimistic, how much of life can you really make in your own image?

Many things don't in the least depend on your will — the facts of nature, the truths of mathematics, the reality of other people. If you try to remake them in your own image, you're just making your life into a lie. You're distorting the world and ignoring the importance and freedom of other people.

The facts known by the sciences are facts whether you want them to be or not. The size and shape of the earth and the solar system are not determined by your free choices. You don't choose to be a living, sensing, thinking thing. It's just what you are. Free choice is good, but it doesn't dictate truth. Truth depends on what is, not on what you choose.

Even social reality can't be made in your image. Your choices contribute to the social order, but many aspects of your life are not in your control — your background, your talents. In addition, there's a world full of human beings with wills of their own. Relationships don't only depend on what you choose; they also depend on the deeds and attitudes of others.

Although much of life is what you make it, the world is not your invention, nor other people mere extensions of yourself. The world, other people, and you, make life what it is.

That reality is "independent" means that
there is something in every experience
that escapes our arbitrary control.
William James
"Humanism and Truth"

89

Live and
let live

I have the right to live my own life without being judged by others. So do you. So does everybody. Life would be a lot better if people weren't judgmental.

Look at the prejudice in the world. It all comes from people being judgmental. They don't understand other people, so they condemn them. Maybe they do it to feel superior, but it's narrow-minded and unjust. Tensions over race, gender, and sexual orientation come from people judging others. We've got to stop condemning and start tolerating each other.

Besides, individuals get hurt when lifestyles are attacked. It's humiliating and debilitating when you're judged to be wrong. You lose confidence in yourself and feel cut off from the community. Each person should be encouraged to pursue his dreams. Judgmental people need to mind their own business and let the rest of us get on with our lives.

I know how we can best end prejudice: let's stop thinking that our way of living is best. Let's give others the benefit of the doubt. Let's *live and let live.*

Is it not better to remain in suspense than to entangle your-self in the many errors that human fancy has produced? Is it not better to suspend your conviction than to get mixed up in these seditious and quarrelsome divisions?
Michel de Montaigne
Apology for Raymond Sebond

I T'S TRUE THAT we have no right to insist that everyone be
just like us. Condemning others just because they're different
is clearly unjust. And many people's lives have been ruined by
prejudice; they've had their opportunities cut off and their
reputations destroyed. But when you condemn those who
are judgmental, aren't you being judgmental yourself?

Is it even possible not to be judgmental? Are you really
willing to tolerate all positions? The rejection of prejudice and
the condemnation of intolerance are themselves judgments.
Judging is inevitable and often right; the problem is not with
making judgments; it's with making wrong judgments.

To avoid making wrong judgments, we've got to do two
things. First, we've got to distinguish the action from the actor.
If an action is wrong, we should condemn it, no matter who
does it. However, a person is not just his actions. We all make
mistakes; but we can repent and change. So, even as we condemn wrong actions, we should never condemn the actors.

Second, we've got to distinguish actions that are morally
wrong from those that are just different from our ways and so
unfamiliar to us. We should only condemn those actions that
are morally wrong. Differences in cultural traditions or religious
practices that do not violate any moral norms should never
be condemned. In fact, we should try to appreciate them.

*People should be allowed to live free from
prejudice, but also free to take responsibility
for their choices. Don't just live and let live:
live well, and help others live well, too.*

*I have deliberately neglected what occupies most people: wealth,
household affairs, power. Instead, I have tried to persuade each
of you not to care for any of his belongings before caring that
he himself should be as good and wise as possible.*
Socrates
in Plato's *Apology,* 36c

Live for
today

Why worry about tomorrow? There's
nothing you can do about it. In the end,
we're all forgotten. Anyway, there's
so much to enjoy here and now.

Look at all the people who work and work and work, and
never get to enjoy the fruits of their labors. They spend years
saving up for retirement and then they die. What a waste!
I'm not getting caught in that trap. I'm not going to spend
my life working like a slave just so I can have a comfortable retirement. Better to enjoy myself while I'm young.

Besides, the present is all we really have. If we live in the
past or for the future, we're missing out on what's really real.
Most importantly, we miss out on the people around us. We
can't really love people if we're distracted by regrets about
the past or obsessed with plans for the future. There won't
ever be another moment like this one. Make the best of it.

Don't get caught worrying about what
might have been. Don't put off having fun
until tomorrow. Celebrate the moment!
It's all we have. *Live for today!*

This music is forever for me. It's the stage
thing, that rush moment you live for.
It never lasts, but that's what you live for.
Bruce Springsteen
Time Magazine, 10/27/1975

I T'S TRUE THAT we can become consumed with our work and preoccupied with planning for the future. We can be so obsessed with tomorrow that we miss out on the good things we have today. We don't know the hour of our death. Piling up riches won't guarantee our security. But can you succeed in enjoying the present if you ignore the past and the future?

We're all creatures of time. We have unique histories leading to the present, histories that are incomplete. Each life is like a story unfolding. Just as a good story has a beginning, a middle, and an end, so each life has a past, a present, and a future. Can you find happiness in isolation from your past and future?

You and your relationships with others are in many ways products of the past. Your knowledge and character arise from your past experiences and choices. Friendships depend, in part, on keeping the past alive. Past pledges of affection and shared experiences bind you and your friends together. Your present enjoyment of each other depends on your past actions.

And if you really care about yourself and your friends, you can't ignore the future. Your life tomorrow depends on your choices today. If you're reckless now, you endanger your future carefree living. True friendships are built on trust, and deep trust requires commitment. Only through a commitment to a future together can your friendship blossom today.

Yes, live for today. But don't forget that your rich life today arises from yesterday's choices. So live now in such a way that tomorrow's today will be as enjoyable as today.

Whatever makes the past, the distant, or the future predominate over the present, advances us in the dignity of thinking beings.
Samuel Johnson
"A Journey to the Western Islands of Scotland"

Look on
the bright side

I'm always optimistic. Might as well be.
After all, what's the alternative? Pessimism
never got anyone anywhere. I believe
that things are going to work out fine.

Depression is the worst threat to happiness. It's miserable
and debilitating. Optimism keeps it away. My optimism
keeps me cheerful and on the lookout for opportunities to
benefit myself. Not only does my optimism help me see new
opportunities; it actually creates them. I find ways to make
good things happen because I believe that they can happen.

My optimism helps others, too. It's infectious. Other people
pick up on it and begin to feel it, too. A common vision of
hope is essential for cooperation on any level. Families
work through tough times when they keep a positive
attitude. Friendships thrive on mutual support. Projects in
the community get done because people are optimistic.

Pessimism kills; optimism gives life. Make your
choice; it's not a hard one. Doom and gloom
get you nowhere. To create a good life and
find happiness, *look on the bright side.*

*Nothing contributes more to cheerfulness than the
habit of looking on the good side of things.*
Archbishop William Ullathorne
Humility and Patience

I T'S TRUE THAT a positive attitude is critical for success. If you think you can't win, you probably won't. Optimism at least gives you a chance. And optimism has a way of strengthening community. One person's optimism gives others a sense that things really matter and that they can make a difference. But can looking on the bright side also sometimes blind us?

Is there a danger that, by trying to put the best spin on things, we'll distort the way things really are? And if we do this, aren't we actually making it harder to succeed? If I think getting an "A" in algebra is easy, I won't study hard enough. I may fail a course that, with some effort, I could have passed.

Looking on the bright side can interfere with knowing the truth about reality and the truth about ourselves. There may be dangers ahead that I should take seriously. Optimism may cause me to ignore them. And if I do see the dangers, I may tell myself that I have the talent and intelligence to overcome them easily. I won't make the necessary effort to prepare myself.

If I am too optimistic about the goodness of other people, I may put myself and others in harm's way. Trusting a liar or a thief is an invitation to deception and loss. It's best to see people as they are, not to overestimate or underestimate their good will and character. Only then can I make the right choice, the one that is best for me and for those for whom I have responsibility.

Initially, looking on the bright side may help us through tough times. But we'll only find real solutions by looking on the right side — by knowing the truth about reality.

Popular optimism is the apotheosis of superficiality. The obvious is its support, the inane its ornament.
Agnes Repplier
Points of Friction

Look out
for number one

Everybody puts himself first. It's the way of the world. You'd be a fool not to care for yourself most of all. If you don't do it, who will?

It's only natural to be concerned first and foremost with yourself. After all, the only person whose desires and needs you're really sure about is you. Once you've addressed these, you may want to turn to others. But even here, you do so because it's something you want to do. There's really no way to avoid putting yourself first. Everybody does it.

Not only is it natural to take care of yourself first, it's also the most efficient way to organize society. It's easier to take care of yourself than to figure out how to meet the desires and needs of another person. So if everybody looks out for himself first, we'll all get along just fine. Then, if we feel like getting together, we'll do so freely and without obligation.

Life would be simple if everyone were self-sufficient. There'd be no need to look out for others if they'd look out for themselves. The key is: you've got to *look out for number one.*

Egoism is so deeply rooted a quality of all individuals in general, that in order to rouse the activity of an individual being, egotistical ends are the only ones upon which we count with certainty.
Arthur Schopenhauer
Supplement to *The World as Will and Idea*

I T'S TRUE THAT we naturally think of ourselves first. We're directly aware of our needs and desires, but only indirectly aware of the desires and needs of others. And there's a lot to be said for the efficiency and freedom of everybody taking care of himself. But is striving to satisfy your own needs and desires actually the best way to take care of yourself?

That is, if you're really serious about making yourself happy, aren't you going about it the wrong way when you just strive to gratify your desires? Think about it. Who are you? Are you just an animal programmed to seek pleasure and avoid pain? Certainly, you're an animal, but aren't you something more?

Isn't it more central to who you are that you think and choose? Unlike the other animals, you ask questions about what's true and wonder about the best way to live. You commit yourself to projects that seem to you worthwhile. You reach out in friendship to others. If you really care about yourself, shouldn't you care most about fulfilling these capacities for purposeful action?

But these are fulfilled by thinking and choosing well, that is, by being wise and good. Look out for these things, and you'll soon be happy. And here's the bonus: you don't have to choose between self and others. It's a win-win situation: both you and others are better off. By becoming wise and good, you help others; and by helping others, you become wise and good.

> *Sure, put yourself first, but deeply, not super-*
> *ficially. To really care about yourself, look for*
> *what's humanly best. Be wise and good and*
> *really look after number one.*

A good man should be a lover of self: he will help himself
to do what is noble and will benefit others; but an evil man
should not, for in following bad passions he will harm
both himself and his neighbors.
Aristotle
Nicomachean Ethics, VIII, 8

Love
is blind

I'm so in love. As far as I can see, she's perfect for me. There's nothing she should change. I don't care what tomorrow may bring as long as we've got each other.

The way I feel, there's nothing I want to do but to be with her. I'd go anywhere just to see her. I'd do anything she asked. I'd stand in the rain, waiting; I'd walk through fire. Say what you want about her defects — I don't see them. She's everything I've ever hoped for and more. It's really love when all you want to do is be together, when all you see is good.

Who cares about the world? Let it go hang. I can't see what the future holds or where I'm going, and I don't care. As long as we have each other, we can face anything. With love, it's clear sailing. Without love, it's hopeless. Don't ask me about the state of the world. I can't see anything or anyone except her. But I don't need to. It's really true: all you need is love.

I have no choice but to go where love leads. She's filled my life with a hope and promise I've never known before. I love her madly. Yes, *love is blind,* and I love it.

L'amour est aveugle; l'amitié ferme les yeux. Love is blind; friendship closes its eyes.
Proverbial saying

I'T'S TRUE THAT love is unconditional devotion. To love is to care for another for the other's own sake, not for what it brings you. Love always sees what's best in the beloved and doesn't dwell on the faults. And love provides a secure center from which to face the future, an oasis the world can't destroy. But if love always turns a blind eye to faults and dangers, how can it grow?

If you really love someone, don't you want that person to be as good as possible? Is it really love to ignore a person's faults? Don't you have to plan for a future together, a future in which your love can spread to family and friends? And don't you have to work at making the world more hospitable to love?

True love loyally supports the beloved, but it doesn't ignore faults. In fact, it sees those faults more clearly than a neutral party would. Love sees those faults as standing in the way of the beloved's full happiness. Love longs to help the beloved overcome the faults — not by direct criticism and coercion, but gently and with kindness, making room for love to grow.

And love can't grow without some vision of a perfect future and hard work to make that future a reality. If you really love someone, you want her to have other friends and a network of support. This means planning for the future and working to build good communities, from your family, to your town, to your nation and the world. Love needs loving support.

Though it sees goodness and promise first, love isn't blind to faults and dangers. Love sees the beloved and the world transformed — the beloved perfected and the world at peace.

Love is not blind; that is the last thing it is. Love is bound; and the more it is bound, the less it is blind.
G. K. Chesterton
Orthodoxy, Ch. 5

Love means never having to say you're sorry

If you're really in love, you don't have to say it. You just know the devotion is there. You know you'll always be forgiven; you don't have to ask for it.

True love is a deep trust and a real "sympatico." It's almost like being one person. You know what the other is thinking even without being told. You're together because it feels right. You don't have to work at it; it's just natural. To analyze each other's motives and responsibilities would ruin the magic of it all. Besides, lovers would never intentionally hurt each other.

And even if they do, they know that they're forgiven. If in the strain of the moment, I'm rude to my beloved, or angry with her, she knows I didn't really mean it. There's no need to say I'm sorry. Your beloved is like a second self. Just as there's no need to apologize to yourself, so there's no need to apologize to your true love. Forgiveness is automatic.

To love is to live as one. Lovers accept each other just as they are. They give, expecting nothing in return. *Love means never having to say you're sorry.*

Love is an endless act of forgiveness,
a tender look which becomes a habit.
Peter Ustinov
Christian Science Monitor, 12/9/1958

I T'S TRUE THAT those in love share a life together in a most intimate way. They often have no need of speech because their thoughts move in the same direction. True love cares more for the beloved than for self, and forgiveness preempts the need for apology. But if you've wronged your beloved, can you really be in love without wanting to say you're sorry?

If you really care for the other more than for yourself, don't you want what's best for the other? Don't you wish that you could do more for the other and regret whatever stands in the way, including your own faults? Can love grow without an ongoing profession of inadequacy and need for forgiveness?

Even though love never intends to harm the beloved, some-times misunderstandings arise. If I've hurt my beloved, she may believe that I'm sorry without my saying so. But if I'm really in love, I want her to know she's loved and that I'm committed, despite my failures, to building up the love we share together. So I search for the words to make this clear.

True love does offer the beloved a kind of guarantee of for-giveness. It doesn't require an apology for the beloved's every shortcoming and mistake: that would be selfish. However, the lover does desire to apologize for his own shortcomings and mistakes, for he knows that these get in the way of a fuller blossoming of the love he treasures.

Indeed, love is never having to say you're sorry, but it's also, and more importantly, always wanting to say you're sorry for all that you've done that puts love in jeopardy.

Teach your children your readiness to apologize for hurt you have inflicted on others.
Lawrence Batler
Not in Front of the Children, Ch. 4

Make love,
not war

War is never the answer. Violence just begets more violence. The only way to put an end to this cycle of violence is to love your enemies.

We're called to love each other. People from other countries are like us. They just want the chance to raise their families in peace and be successful. The only reason they fight is because they can't live in basic human dignity. Instead of fighting them, we should try to find out what they need and then help them get it. Only then will we have real peace.

Plus, retaliation and revenge are always immoral. You should never intentionally do what you know to be wrong. But we all know that killing other people is wrong. So we should never do it, even when someone has harmed us. After all, two wrongs don't make a right. Just because someone else has tried to hurt us, that doesn't give us the right to hurt them.

Don't try to defeat violence with violence. It'll never work. You can't force people to be good. You have to show them you really care about them. *Make love, not war.*

Can anything be more ridiculous than that a man should have the right to kill me because he lives on the other side of the water, and because his ruler has a quarrel with mine, though I have none with him?
Blaise Pascal
Pensées, V, 294

I T'S TRUE THAT, all things being equal, we should seek to love others rather than fight them. Love is better than hate; helping others is better than hurting them. And mutual understanding goes a long way toward diffusing fear and animosity, thus preventing or ending war and violence. But is it really love to turn your back on injustice in the name of nonviolence?

I may decide not to fight someone who attacks me. Though I have a right to defend myself, I'm not wrong to choose pacifism. But may I stand by and do nothing if he attacks my daughter or my neighbor's daughter? Or may a powerful nation do nothing while innocent nations are unjustly invaded?

Is it enough for us simply not to do evil? Or are we required to fight against evil? Do we have obligations to help others? If someone is being raped, and I can do something about it, I can't just mind my own business. Clearly, I should step in to prevent the injustice. We have a duty to protect the innocent. We've got to stand up to evil to make the world safe for love.

Maybe we think the love and forgiveness that we show aggressors by not fighting them makes up for our failure to defend the innocent. But do you really help people by letting them get away with evil? Won't they just get worse? The worst thing is to be confirmed in evil. Punishment gives the enemy the opportunity to face up to his evil and to turn away from it.

Love is a moral ideal; war is not. But to make room for love, the injustice in us and in our enemies must be defeated. When you fight for justice, make love, not war, your aim.

We do not seek peace in order to be at war, but we go to war that we may have peace. Be peaceful, therefore, in warring, so that you may vanquish those whom you war against and bring them to the prosperity of peace.
St. Augustine
Letter 189 to Boniface

Might
makes right

People with power make the rules. What mom and dad said was law. Teachers could punish all of us just because a few acted up. It's always been that way.

When you grow up, you find that the whole world operates this way. Because they have a badge, police can pull you over and hassle you for no good reason. Dictators like Hitler and Stalin use political and military power to oppress and indoctrinate people. Those with "might" conquer other lands and then use their power to whitewash what they've done.

Even in a democracy, power rules. The party in control of the government makes the laws that say what's right and what's wrong. Depending on who's in power, things like gambling and prostitution are wrong in one state and right in another. What's right is simply what's legal, and those who have power at the moment decide what that will be.

Those who can impose their power, will. Power makes the laws, and the laws say what's right and wrong. It's just a fact of life: *might makes right.*

The victor will not be asked whether he told the truth or not. In war, it is not Right that matters but Victory. Have no pity. Adopt a brutal attitude. Right is on the side of the strongest.
Adolf Hitler
Speech, 8/22/1939

I T'S TRUE THAT those in power often get their way. Parents have power over children, teachers over students, and bureaucrats over citizens. Dictators impose laws on their people. And even in a free society like ours, the power of the majority rules. But if you really think that power is the source of right and wrong, can you legitimately object to arbitrary impositions of power?

If you think that power determines what's just, how can you ever judge that any punishment is undeserved or that a parent or policeman wields power unjustly? Why should dictators who have power treat their subjects fairly? If right depends on might, is it even possible for any action to be unjust?

If might literally makes right, then whatever happens is right. By your standard, because Hitler had the power to carry them out, his actions were not wrong. Because slavery was imposed by those in power, it wasn't wrong. Nor were these actions even illegal at the time. The Nazis acted in accord with the law, and so did American slave owners before the Civil War.

But the Nazis were rightly convicted for violating a more basic law, a natural law that might does not create and that might cannot change. Because of this natural law, it was right to punish the Nazis, and right to outlaw slavery. Some things, like genocide and slavery, are obviously wrong. You can know this by putting yourself in the other person's shoes.

Sometimes laws are merely the products of power, but laws should be grounded in justice. Rather than might making right, right should guide might.

I believe that unarmed truth and unconditional love will have the final word in reality. This is why right, temporarily defeated, is stronger than evil triumphant.
Martin Luther King, Jr.
Accepting Nobel Peace Prize, 12/10/1964

My country, right or wrong

Patriotism is the duty of every citizen. We must defend our country against all enemies. Times of crisis demand wholehearted allegiance, not criticism.

People naturally love their homeland. It's where they grew up. It's what they know. It's hard to imagine it being any other way. We owe so much to our country — our education, our freedoms, our opportunities. But if we're not willing to defend our country, these freedoms and opportunities we take for granted could easily be taken away. We can't let this happen.

Just as the first duty of government is to protect us, so our first duty to our nation is its defense. Loyalty is a great virtue. We don't limit our loyalty to family members to the times when they are perfect. We stand by each other through thick and thin. Neither should we limit our patriotism to those times when we're sure our country is right.

We've got to stand together in defense of our country. If we don't, we'll lose the privileges our country has given us. Unconditional loyalty is a must. *My country, right or wrong!*

It is the duty of a patriot to prefer and promote the exclusive interest and glory of his native country.
Edward Gibbon
Decline and Fall of the Roman Empire

IT'S TRUE THAT we owe much to our nation in terms of freedom and opportunities. We should never forget the sacrifices of those who made these freedoms and opportunities possible. And patriotism, like loyalty, is not just for the good times. But if "friends don't let friends drive drunk," should patriots stand by idly when their country does grievous wrong?

That's like arbitrarily preferring yourself over everyone else — not because you're better, but simply because you're you. Such preference is incompatible with moral responsibility. But neither is our country good just because it's our country. May we ignore or even accept its flaws in the name of patriotism?

In WWII, the Germans and the Japanese loved their countries, but that hardly justified their attacks on other countries, nor their citizens' support for such attacks. Indeed, if every country adopts it, "my country right or wrong" will prove a recipe for perpetual war. No country will admit its errors, and citizens will never be justified in opposing bad decisions by their governments.

If our country's policies are flawed, we should try to get them changed. We should do everything in our power to make our nation worthy of defending. Nor is this unpatriotic. In fact, it's quite the contrary. Just as trying to prevent a friend from doing wrong is a sign of true friendship, so trying to prevent our country from doing wrong is a sign of true patriotism.

> *Although we should stand by our country even when mistakes are made, we should always strive to turn "my country right or wrong" into "my country right."*

He alone is a patriot who will suffer obliquy and loss of money and friends, rather than betray truth, justice, and righteousness. Only by fidelity to these can he rightly serve his country.
Archbishop J. L. Spalding
Opportunity and Other Essays

Necessity
knows no law

In good times, it's easy to follow the moral law. But in tough times, you have to make exceptions. When push comes to shove, you just have to do what you have to do.

Take stealing, for example. Almost everyone thinks stealing is a bad idea. Since we don't want others to steal from us, we understand why we shouldn't steal from them. But if you're starving and have no money for food, it's a different story. You have to steal. If you don't, you'll die. Everybody agrees that, in such desperate straits, stealing is O.K.; in fact it's necessary.

Or what about killing? Normally, of course, you shouldn't go around killing people. But suppose you're attacked and the only way to save your life is to kill the attacker. Should you do nothing and let him kill you? Of course not. You have every right to kill the attacker in order to preserve your life. The law against killing is overruled by the necessity of the moment.

The strict moral law is fine for those who are comfortable. But put someone in a threatening situation, and morality goes out the window. *Necessity knows no law.*

*Morality is a private
and costly luxury.*
Henry Adams
The Education of Henry Adams, Ch. 22

I T'S TRUE THAT extreme situations often test the clarity of moral principles. Moral prohibitions against stealing and lying are easy to follow in times of peace and prosperity, but seem hard to honor under life-threatening conditions. It seems, then, that every moral law has its exceptions. But can anything ever justify abandoning the duty always to do good and avoid evil?

Could you say it's sometimes good to do what's evil? But this is an obvious contradiction. It's possible that man-made laws could be set aside in extreme situations of need or danger; but it's not possible that you could ever be free from the obligation to do what's right. This law knows no exceptions.

Indeed, what seem to be exceptions aren't. To see this we have to focus on what's morally essential to an action. If an action is to be blamed or praised, it must be deliberate. Only intentional actions can be morally good or bad. We don't blame the baby for pulling her brother's hair, for she doesn't mean to. She's not intentionally trying to hurt her brother.

Apply this to killing in self-defense. Killing in the strict sense is the deliberate choice to end life. But "killing in self-defense" isn't so much choosing to end life as it is choosing to save life. You don't really want to kill the attacker; you just want to protect yourself. Your act of self-defense, even though it kills, isn't intended to take life. If it were, it would be wrong.

> *Extraordinary circumstances challenge the absolute character of the moral law. But the law against intentionally choosing evil knows no exceptions, however dire the necessity.*

The moral principles excluding revenge by any means and unfairness in any form are absolutes.
John Finnis
Moral Absolutes, Ch. 3, Sec. 2

Nice guys finish last

Don't fall for that "nice guy" stuff. All you get from it is insult and injury. If you give 'em the chance, they'll take advantage of you. Never give a sucker an even break.

It's a tough world out there. The competition is fierce. If you want to succeed, it's got to be full throttle from the word "go." There are only a couple of places on the team for newcomers, and you can't allow the other guy to get more attention than you. If you do, you'll be forgotten. It's the same thing in business. You've got to be aggressive and put yourself first.

If you do give people a break, they'll walk all over you. This is the story of mankind. Socrates tried to be fair and reasonable, seeking truth and virtue over power and protection. What did he get for his pains? They made him drink the hemlock. Jesus tried to be nice, and look what they did to him. Whatever you do in life, you can't be "Mr. Nice Guy" and come out on top.

If you want to get the most out of life, you have to be willing to take what you can get, by hook or crook. If you don't, someone else will. *Nice guys finish last.*

Right, as the world goes, is only in question between equals in power, while the strong do what they can do and the weak suffer what they must.
Thucydides
Peloponnesian War, V, 89

I T'S TRUE THAT you've got to work hard to succeed in this world. In our democratic and capitalist system, you only get out what you put in. Those who compete fiercely reap the rewards of their efforts. Those who step back to give others a shot weaken their own chances for success. But is being first in wealth, power, and fame the last word on victory and success?

There's nothing wrong with the so-called goods of fortune: wealth, power, glory, and fame. Getting them is a kind of success. If you take advantage of your opportunities and other people, you'll likely get more of these goods. But are these goods the only things you want? And do you want them most?

If so, then being nice might get in your way. In a soccer game, refusing to foul your opponent though she fouls you can mean defeat. Pointing out an inequity to the other party in a business contract can cost you real money. But what about things like virtue, friendship, and peace? Don't you want them, too? What good are money and fame if you don't have friends?

The goods of fortune are notoriously fickle. You can earn money fast and lose it even faster; you can be famous one day and forgotten the next. But friendship and virtue are long-lasting. Honesty, patience, and generosity belong to you intimately and can't be taken away. To get them, you only have to practice them: to be thoughtful, kind, and loving — to be "nice."

It may be true that, in the race for fame and fortune, nice guys finish last. But it's not so in the search for the goods that last. Here, to be first in love, is to finish first.

Let us have the faith that right makes might, and in that faith, let us, to the end, dare to do our duty as we understand it.
Abraham Lincoln
Speech, 2/27/1860

Nothing is good or bad but thinking makes it so

Reality is value-free. Our world is just the product of unthinking evolution. Values are nothing but the inventions of human beings.

Water doesn't flow because it thinks flowing is good. Trees don't grow and reproduce out of a sense of duty. Animals don't take responsibility for their actions, and they're not bothered by guilty consciences. We may think there's an objective natural order: that plants are better than rocks, animals better than plants, and humans better than all the rest. But it's not so.

We just impose our subjective values on the world and on each other. People who are easily influenced accept the values of those who are more confident. Those who are aggressive do their best to make everyone else accept their values. Because of their success, it may seem that there are objective moral norms. But there are no values that we all hold naturally.

Good and bad are not found in Nature. They're products of the human desire for pleasure and power. Clearly, *nothing is good or bad but thinking makes it so.*

Man is the measure of all things, of things that are as they are, and of things that are not what they are not.
Protagoras
Fragment 1

IT'S TRUE THAT nature doesn't seem to follow moral laws. Rocks, plants, and animals don't act out of concern for what's good. Values are found only among human beings, and they're often manipulated for advantage rather than honored as objective moral guides. But if thinking simply invents good and bad, what's wrong with me arbitrarily choosing to ignore what you say?

Why should I accept your claim that everything is just the product of unthinking evolution? First off, if your thoughts are just the products of blind chance, what possible reason can you have to think they're true? Would you trust a road map that was drawn up by a computer programmed by a hail storm?

Secondly, why should I value your thoughts more than mine? Presumably, you make your point because you believe that it's better than what I think and that I ought to agree with you. Otherwise, there's no purpose in your communicating your position. But why should I bother to consider your point as better than mine if better is just a matter of my interpretation?

To make a moral judgment, you must believe in moral norms that hold for everyone. If you will that good and bad should be matters of personal interpretation, then you are also willing that any interpretation of them is legitimate. This includes the one that rejects your point, but also those that think you should be cheated, lied to, or killed. I don't will these; neither do you.

In the sense that only those who think can
know them, good and bad depend on thinking.
But moral thinking is only possible because
knowledge of good and bad makes it so.

Whatever we can say in all truth is commended
by its own good nature, even if not approved
by any man living.
Cicero
On Moral Duties, Bk. 1, Ch. 4

One man's heaven
is another man's hell

People are different. There's no view
you can think of that doesn't have its
defenders. What some think is the worst
way of life, others honor as the best.

It's like Br'er Rabbit and the briar patch. The fox thought that
the worst punishment would be to throw Brer Rabbit in the briar
patch. But it turns out he doesn't mind the briar patch: in fact,
he loves it. So it is with us. You may think that a life devoted
to rap music would be the last thing you'd want, but to me
it's the best. To me, books like this one are deadly dull.

Consider suicide bombers. To most of us, suicide bombers
commit the two worst possible actions: they kill innocent
people and they kill themselves. But to the bombers themselves and their supporters, their actions are heroic, deserving
of heaven. They believe that they're doing two great things:
killing the enemy, and sacrificing their lives for God.

There is no heavenly ideal. Happiness
means different things to different people.
Opposite values find loyal defenders. Truly,
one man's heaven is another man's hell.

What's one man's poison is
another's meat and drink.
Beaumont and Fletcher
Love's Cure, Act 3, Sc. 2

I T'S TRUE THAT not all people agree about what counts as ultimate happiness or heaven. Some things are just matters of taste, like what kind of car or clothes would make you happy. Others are matters of loyalty, such as whose family, or school, or nation is the best. But since no one thinks of heaven as bad or hell as good, don't we have grounds for some basic agreement?

There's at least wide agreement on what would not be heaven. Would being constantly ill and in pain be anyone's ideal? What about being tortured forever? Or how about being universally hated and persecuted? No one thinks that these miserable states would be heavenly. Here's some agreement.

Besides these physical and external miseries, there are internal states of mind that no one would desire. Who wants to be always deceived about the nature of reality or about the fidelity and trustworthiness of friends? Who wants to be a mere puppet manipulated by someone else's whims? A life of forced ignorance and enslavement is nobody's idea of heaven.

More positively, our idea of ultimate happiness includes the enrichment of our lives. Happiness is not just freedom from pain, injury, and disease; it's also health. Happiness includes, not just the absence of propaganda and coercion, but knowing the truth and choosing freely to join a community of friends where justice reigns.

> People may have different tastes and preferences, but no one prefers a hell of suffering, ignorance, and slavery over a heaven of healing, knowledge, and freedom.

Just as nobody wants not to exist, so nobody wants not to be happy.
St. Augustine
City of God, Bk. 11, Ch. 26

Power corrupts

Most people are basically good. They're brought up to be cooperative and to fit in with society. But give people power, and watch how quickly they turn bad.

Just look around. What's the general track record of humanity? Every time people have enough power to do what they want to do, they go wrong. As soon as children are strong enough to disobey and to get away with it, they do. People who are honest and kind in their families and communities take advantage of others when they're given the power to do so.

And think of examples from history. It didn't take long for the power of the Roman emperors to corrupt them. It was only a couple of generations from noble Augustus to corrupt Nero. Think of the corruption of modern tyrants — Hitler, Stalin, Saddam Hussein. Their power led them to all sorts of excesses and injustices. People simply cannot handle power.

There seems to be an inverse proportion between power and virtue: the more power people have, the less virtuous they become. *Power corrupts.*

The effect of power and publicity on all men is the aggravation of self, a sort of tumor that ends by killing the victim's sympathies.
Henry Adams
The Education of Henry Adams, Ch. 10

I T'S TRUE THAT lack of power restrains most of us. Certainly, we desire to do some things of which society disapproves. Knowing that we can't get away with them keeps us from attempting them. And it's remarkable how many past leaders became unjust once they gained power. But does power cause this tendency toward injustice or just permit it?

If it causes it, then wherever we find great power we'll find great injustice. But that's not the case. Parents have great power over their children, but most don't abuse it. Teachers have power over students and doctors over patients, but most teachers and doctors are honest and caring, not deceitful and corrupt.

At worst, power is morally neutral. The injustice of the powerful is a result of how they use their power, not the power itself. Powerful people can refuse to take advantage of the weak and defenseless. We can refuse to lie or take what's not ours, even if we have the power to do so and not get caught. A good person uses power for good; a bad person uses it for evil.

In fact, power is good. Without it, we can't do anything. We can't carry out good plans, like getting an education, expanding our artistic and cultural horizons through travel, or supporting a family. Without power, we can't help the powerless. If we're going to feed the hungry, aid the poor, heal the sick, and defend the innocent, we need power. Without power, no good is done.

Power gives us opportunities: it's up to us to decide how to use them. With power, we can do great things, or we can inflict enormous harm. Bad choices corrupt people, not power.

Power does not corrupt men. But fools, if they get into a position of power, corrupt power.
George Bernard Shaw
in Stephen Winsten's *Days with Bernard Shaw*

The proof
is in the pudding

Results don't lie. If something's right, it
brings good consequences. You can know
the quality of a tree by its fruit. Good
ideas and good actions bear good fruit.

This is the foundation of the scientific and technological
revolution. A true hypothesis is proven by experimental data.
New ideas in medicine are good only if they heal people. A
good technological insight is one that leads to new and
useful products to make our lives better. The microchip's value
is clear from its enormous benefits for storing information.

The same is true for personal judgments and political solutions.
We have lots of ideas; the good ones lead to some productive
end. The bad ones turn out to be useless. Political ideas are a
dime a dozen; the good ones are revealed by their results,
whether in improved economic growth, better care of the poor,
or successful foreign policy. The bad ones produce nothing.

There are lots of ideas out there, all claiming
to be true. There's only one sure way to sort
them out — results. Good ideas have good
consequences. *The proof is in the pudding.*

*"The true", to put it very briefly, is only the expedient
in the way of our thinking, just as "the right" is only
the expedient in the way of our behaving.*
William James
Pragmatism

I T'S TRUE THAT right ideas and good actions normally have good consequences and that good consequences are often reliable indicators of the truth and goodness of ideas. This is the case for science and technology, as it is for many of the moral and political ideas that guide our lives. But if goodness is solely a matter of results, how can I know what to do before I act?

What works for science and technology doesn't seem to fit moral and political choices. In science, truth always awaits the verification of hypotheses. At first I only hypothesize that in a vacuum a feather will fall at the same rate as a rock. After the experiment has confirmed my hypothesis, I know that it's true.

But this method won't work for moral action. We're obliged to choose only good actions. But if I can't know that what I do is good until the results of my actions are in, how can I ever, with a clear conscience, do anything? After all, the results of my choice might be bad. But I can't know ahead of time. Results just aren't a practical way of evaluating moral actions.

Nor are they a moral way — unless we're prepared to say that intentions don't matter. If only results count, intentionally killing an innocent person might not be wrong. We'll just have to wait and see whether the consequences are good or bad. But since deliberately killing innocent people can't ever be right, results alone don't prove an act to be right or wrong.

Scientific or economic proof is in the pudding since the results verify the hypothesis. But in ethics, good results don't always mean good intentions, so the pudding alone is no proof.

Moral value does not depend on achieving the objective for which we are acting; instead, moral value depends on the principle on which the will chooses to act.
Immanuel Kant
Foundations of the Metaphysics of Morals, Section 1

Prove it!

You say there's objective reality: prove it! You say we have an obligation to be good: prove it! You say love is more than physical attraction: prove it!

You can't expect me to agree with you without proof: that would be irrational. Proof is necessary in all areas. If you want me to agree with an algebraic equation, you show me the proof. If it works, I agree with you. If you want me to agree with your claim about the chemical makeup of certain organisms, show me the analysis and experimental data.

Even in the area of morality and politics, we expect proof. No one is convicted in a court of law without evidence. You have to establish the facts and the motives. Personal morality is no different. If lying is wrong, why is it wrong? We don't just accept any political ideal. We want to know why it's a good idea, and whether or not it will really work.

I never accept anything without proof. If you're going to convince me, you're going to have to produce sufficient evidence. *You've got to prove it.*

It is wrong always, everywhere, and for anyone, to believe anything upon insufficient evidence.
W. K. Clifford
"The Ethics of Belief"

IT'S TRUE THAT human understanding advances through proof. Without proof, we're left with irrational preferences. Agreement would be established by force, not reason. Modern science has built up a wealth of information by relying on hypothesis and verification. We look to proof to settle moral and legal issues. But if everything must be proven, can anything be proven?

If everything must be proven, then any claim whatsoever can be challenged. But if every claim can be challenged, how can we get started in formulating our proof? If you and I agree on nothing, then there's no way for me to prove something to you. You could always say, "Prove to me that proof is possible."

Some things can't be proven — not because they're uncertain, but because they're obvious. They're not conclusions; they're directly evident. We don't prove them; we see them. You don't prove that there's a real world and we can know it; you see it. If we disagree about these things, we can't prove anything to each other. But there are no good reasons to disagree about them.

There are similar unproven, self-evident starting points for moral thinking. You can't prove that we have an obligation to be good, nor that we're free to respond to that obligation. That is, you can't point to anything more basic and obvious from which to deduce these things. But you don't need to; these truths are self-evident. There are no good reasons to disagree about them.

> *Proof is invaluable in our cooperative pursuit of truth and virtue. But to demand a proof for the self-evident starting points of thought and choice is irrational and unwarranted.*

If nothing is self-evident, nothing can be proven. Similarly, if nothing is obligatory for its own sake, nothing is obligatory at all.
C. S. Lewis
The Abolition of Man, Ch. 2

Read the signs
of the times

Get with it. Get up to date. Can't you see
which way the wind's blowing? You'd
better learn to read the signs of the times.
If you don't, you'll lose touch with reality.

Look at the computer industry. It's the wave of the future.
If you don't keep up with the latest technology, you'll find
yourself left behind. This is true for individuals as well as
corporations. Students need computers to keep up in
school. Businesses can't be competitive without constant
upgrades. This is the way the world is going. Get on board.

The same is true with moral questions. Every age has a kind
of world spirit, a particular atmosphere that dominates. In
Roman times, it was the spirit of empire. In the Middle Ages,
it was the spirit of religious belief. In the Renaissance, it was
the spirit of adventure and discovery. Today it's the spirit of
freedom — in ideas, politics, economics, and morality.

Be realistic. You can't fight the spirit of the
age; you've got to adjust to it. If you don't,
there's no way you'll be successful. Get with
the program. *Read the signs of the times.*

*Nothing else in the world, not all
the armies, is so powerful as an
idea whose time has come.*
Victor Hugo
The Future of Man

I T'S TRUE THAT trends develop in technology, business, and culture; and they often challenge the ways we've always done things. If you don't spot these trends and keep up with them, you'll fall behind or get left out altogether. It pays to watch out for these directing signs. But is reading the signs of the times really important or itself just a sign of our times?

It does seem important for technology and business. To succeed in these areas, you've got to be in the vanguard. Success comes to the inventor and the entrepreneur. But even here, isn't it the person who's not following signs but thinking outside the box, who's really in the vanguard?

Isn't this true of science, too? Rather than following the trends of his time, the great scientist focuses on making the most sense out of the evidence. This is what Copernicus did; this is what Einstein did. Ignoring fads, the great scientist looks for the best explanation for the way the world really is. Because of this focus on evidence, he ends up changing the times.

The same thing's true of morality. Sure, there's a moral drift to culture just as there's a direction to the trends in fashion. But you're not bound to follow such a drift; you have free choice. Should you follow? That depends on the moral evidence. If the direction is good, follow; if it's bad, don't. The moral future is not fixed by our times but is waiting to be freely created.

Sure, every time has its signs; but a sign is not a certainty, nor a clear guide for action. So don't follow signs: use your reason to follow evidence, and change the times for the better.

When a prodigy appears or you regard an omen, superstition is at your side. And since such signs are usually all around us, no one who believes them can have peace of mind.
Cicero
Divination, II, 72

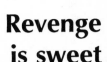

Revenge is sweet

Oh, it feels so good when those who've hurt you get what's coming to them. It just wouldn't be fair for them to get away with it. Injustice must never go unpunished.

We feel a real sense of psychological and emotional healing when those who mistreat us are punished. We hear this all the time from the victims of abuse or the relatives of people who have been murdered. When the criminals are finally punished, they say they can finally get on with their lives. They're comforted knowing that hurt has been met with hurt.

It's also a matter of justice. It's only fair that those who have harmed others should suffer harm themselves. If they didn't, the balance in society would be upset. When something has been taken away from society (whether it's property, human dignity, or life), order is only restored when something is given back — value for value, dignity for dignity, life for life.

There's nothing like the feeling you get from seeing bad people get their just deserts. It's a great pleasure to know that they suffered, too. *Revenge is sweet.*

Perish the universe, so long as I have my revenge.
Cyrano de Bergerac
La Mort d'Agrippine

I T'S TRUE THAT injustice should never be countenanced. Some kind of retribution is required. If the moral order has been disrupted, it needs to be restored. Psychological, emotional, physical, and mental harm must be addressed. Not to do so ignores the demands of justice and human decency. But can revenge deliver the sweet peace and justice it promises?

Can feelings of hatred and cruelty bring us peace? If we let hatred and the desire to see someone suffer guide us, there are no limits on our responses. Seeking gratification of emotions rather than fairness, we lose sight of what could justify punishment — the restoration of peace in the community.

Unlike justice, revenge repays harm with harm, regardless of whether the initial harm was freely intended or was the result of an accident. So the mafia man deliberately runs over the child of a neighbor who accidentally ran over his child while backing out of his driveway. Justice, on the other hand, does not repay pain with pain; it simply inflicts punishment where it is due.

Moreover, revenge tends toward escalation. Whether the feuds are between gangs or nations, the idea is the same. "Since we're better than they are, they deserve to suffer twice as much as we have. They killed one of us, we'll take out two of them." Since such escalation seeks to inflict more harm than was suffered, its focus is cruelty, not fairness. In short, it's unjust.

> *Revenge may taste sweet, but it embitters the soul and poisons society. Justice may be less pleasing to the palate, but it heals society and nourishes the soul.*

Revenge is a kind of wild justice; which the more man's nature runs to, the more ought law to weed it out.
Francis Bacon
Essays, 13

Rules are made to be broken

Rules, rules, rules. There are rules for everything, from constitutional law to table manners. But no rule is absolute. All rules should be broken at some time.

There are rules, in the form of skills and strategies, which coaches teach to their players. But the best players bend and may even break these rules when the time's right; that's what makes them great. The same is true for the arts. There are rules of harmony in music and of structure in painting that are traditional, but the masters break them. This isn't fault, but genius.

Even legal rules are made to be broken. Laws are made for the good of social harmony. Sure, most of the time, you should obey them. But if a law tells you to do something that's wrong, then you should break it. So laws that arbitrarily curtail human rights should be broken. Civil disobedience was the appropriate response to the segregation laws of the 1950s.

Don't be a stickler for the rules. If you are, you'll miss out on the higher achievements of spontaneity and creativity. Always remember: *rules are made to be broken.*

Rules are not necessarily sacred;
principles are.
Franklin D. Roosevelt
Speech, 8/24/1935

I T'S TRUE THAT rules don't cover everything we do. Human activities are complex and open to improvement. A slavish devotion to rules can impede such improvement. So sometimes rules should be bent and even broken. But if you think that "rules are made to be broken," how can you avoid either contradicting yourself or recommending anarchy?

Don't you have to follow rules of grammar and logic even to present your ideas? If you don't, no one will understand you. And is it even possible to argue for a moral position without accepting some sort of rule? After all, your point about not being fanatical about rules is itself a kind of norm or rule.

So clearly not all rules are made to be broken. Some have to be followed if you're going to perform any kind of meaningful activity. And if you want to perform it well, there will be other rules. If all the players ignore the coach's rules for improving skill and strategy, you have a pretty sorry team. If all harmony and structure are ignored, music and art are indecipherable.

Nor are all moral rules made to be broken. Sometimes a higher rule takes precedence over a lower. So, if segregation is legal, the rule requiring you to treating people fairly takes precedence over laws against civil disobedience. But some rules, such as the rule about being fair, should never be broken. There's no higher moral rule that could ever justify the choice to be unjust.

Rules that are useful guidelines can be broken, and rules that violate a higher rule should be broken. But the ultimate rules of thought and morality should never be broken.

Law and order make rough things smooth, weaken violence, and stop the anger of painful strife.
Solon
Fragment 5

Seeing
is believing

What I want is concrete proof. It's just
naïve to believe in something that can't
be verified. If you want me to accept
what you say, show me the evidence.

There are lots of ideas floating around which are never backed
up by evidence. People talk about the existence of God, but
they don't have any concrete proof. Or they make much of
the dignity of the human soul, but fail to give any physical
evidence that we even have a soul. Some insist on the reality
of moral absolutes such as justice, but who's ever seen them?

The one thing we are sure of is the physical world. We can
see it, hear it, touch it. All reality ultimately comes down to
sense experience of one kind or another. Even when we're
dealing with particles too small to see, we can set up experi-
ments to test our theories using fine instruments. Then we can
read the results of our experiment, and see for ourselves.

Don't talk to me of ideas that go beyond
our material world. Why should I listen
to such drivel? I'll believe you when you
show me the evidence. *Seeing is believing.*

*All good intellects have repeated, since Bacon's
time, that there can be no real knowledge
but that which is based on observed facts.*
Auguste Comte
Positive Philosophy, Introduction, I

I T'S TRUE THAT physical evidence is one of the strongest reasons we can have to believe in the existence of something. We are absolutely certain of the existence of the material world. We see it, hear it, and touch it. It's wonderful to see what science has learned about the material world. But is there any physical evidence to prove that only physical evidence is conclusive?

What happens to thought if we insist on physical evidence? Where have we seen the axioms of geometry? Where have we touched the principles of logic that make coherent thought possible? What happens to freedom of choice if we hold to this model? Can we physically measure someone's responsibility?

There are some things that we know to be true even though we can't see them. We're sure that "2+2=4"; but we have no empirical verification of the idea of equality. We're sure that it's wrong to murder innocent children, but the wrongness of murder is not a material thing. Some of the most important things — truth and justice — are not verifiable by the senses.

Not only are there some things that we believe but do not see; there are also some that we'll see only if we believe. Take artistic creation or friendship. We don't know ahead of time that we'll produce a poem or a painting. We don't know ahead of time whether a friendship will grow. If we don't believe in the possibility of these things, they will never come to be.

Seeing is certainly one reason for believing. But some of the things we believe don't have their origin in sense experience, and others we can see only because we believe.

The highest truths have no outward image of themselves visible to man. Immaterial things, which are the noblest and the greatest, are shown only in thought and idea.
Plato
Statesman, 286a

Talk
is cheap

Don't just say you care — show me!
Don't tell me what should be
done — do it! It's easy to talk
the talk, but can you walk the walk?

Lots of people can tell you what should be done. It's not hard
to have opinions. They're a dime a dozen. But real leaders
don't just talk; they lead by example. The best captain of a
sports team doesn't just tell you what to do; he shows the
way by practicing what he preaches. The best employer not
only commands, but works harder than her employees.

To talk about reform is one thing; to make reform a reality
is quite another. It's not enough to say what's good; you've
got to put it into practice. The world is full of moralists
ready and willing to tell you what to do, but how many of
them actually do it? We don't need armchair philosophers or
Monday-morning quarterbacks. We need doers, not talkers.

It's easy to talk about what should be
done. But unless you're willing to put your
money where your mouth is, it doesn't
really matter what you say. *Talk is cheap.*

*They who give utterance to words of holy preaching
should first be awake in the earnest practice of good
works, lest, being themselves slack in performing
them, they stir up others by words only.*
Pope St. Gregory I
Pastoral Care, 3, 40

I T'S TRUE THAT there's a world of difference between saying what should be done and doing it. In many activities, the real payoff comes in putting into practice what you preach. The really good person not only says what is good, but does it. But if talk is so cheap, how come so many have been persecuted and even killed because they wouldn't stop talking?

Consider the example of Socrates. He practiced what he preached. He insisted that we should always be good, even if it might lead to our suffering. He challenged his fellow citizens to put virtue before wealth and power. They didn't want to hear it, so they executed him. Talk was not cheap for Socrates.

And what about Martin Luther King, Jr.? Sure, he was a man of action. He led marches in dangerous situations. He organized protests against discrimination. But what he said was even more effective in galvanizing the civil rights movement. His speeches were threatening to many and led to his assassination. It's hard to believe that for Dr. King talk was cheap.

Not only was speaking out costly in effort and danger for Socrates and Martin Luther King, Jr.; it was also more effective than anything else they could have done. Without Socrates, western civilization would look very different today. Without Dr. King's eloquence, the civil rights movement might have failed or taken a more violent turn. Words have power.

Talk is cheap when you don't have to stand by your words; but speaking the truth when those around you don't want to hear it is not. In fact, it may cost you everything.

"Are you a Christian?" said Hilarianus, the governor. And I said, "Yes, I am." Then Hilarianus passed sentence on all of us: we were to be condemned to the beasts.
St. Perpetua
The Martydom of St. Perpetua and Felicitas

There's no accounting for taste

Good taste in art is as hard to pin down as good taste in food. People are different and they like different things. No one can say whose taste is better.

Just as we like different ice-cream flavors, so we like different kinds of art. No one really thinks that the person who likes chocolate better than strawberry has better taste in ice cream. We just have different tastes, that's all. And it doesn't matter. Likewise, we have different tastes in art, music, and literature. The fact that our tastes differ here really doesn't matter, either.

Only snobs think their good taste is really better than the taste of others. They think they have a privileged outlook on the world and are able to distinguish the more beautiful from the less beautiful in some absolute way. They look upon those who disagree as barbarians. It's an elitist position, based more on their social position than their good taste in art.

Taste in art is as democratic as taste in food. There are no clear criteria to rate the various preferences. So everyone's vote counts equally. *There's no accounting for taste.*

These questions of taste, of feeling, of inheritance, need no settlement. Everyone carries his own rule of taste, and amuses himself by applying it, triumphantly, wherever he travels.
Henry Adams
The Education of Henry Adams, Ch. 12

IT'S TRUE THAT taste in art varies widely, almost as widely as taste in food. This is simply a fact that must be admitted. And the snobbery of some people who are proud of their good taste is hard to take. After all, it's not a moral issue. But if there's no accounting for taste, how do you explain the refinements of taste that all of us go through at some time in some way?

Perhaps it's as basic as developing taste for a certain sport. Why does this happen? In the first place, we learn to understand and hence appreciate the complexity of the sport. The more we know about the skills and strategy required to play the sport well, the more we have a taste for that sport.

Even taste in food can be developed. A fine steak cooked at a gourmet French restaurant tastes better than a fast-food hamburger. A fifty-dollar bottle of wine tastes better than a four-dollar bottle. There's nothing really esoteric about this. You can simply tell the difference. You can learn to appreciate good food and wine just as you can learn to appreciate a sport.

So, too, you can develop your taste in art, music, or literature. You can learn to appreciate the subtlety of shape and color in a Rembrandt painting. You can learn to appreciate the intricate rhythms and harmonies of a Mozart symphony. You can learn to hear and appreciate the beauty of Shakespeare's English. In short, you can develop your taste — you can make it better.

It's hard to account for the variety in artistic taste. But since our appreciation can be refined, there must be some standards of beauty to account for our improvement in taste.

Good taste is much more a matter of discrimination than of exclusion, and when good taste feels compelled to exclude, it is with regret, not with pleasure.
W. H. Auden
The Dyer's Hand

There's nothing new under the sun

It's all been done before. Fashions come and go, and then return. Philosophies rehash the same problems and reach the same solutions. History repeats itself.

Of course, it's true that science and technology develop new methods and products, but in the realm of basic ideas and moral principles, it's just a cycle of repetition. Some people think reality is material, others think it's spiritual. Some say we should act on feelings, pursuing pleasure; others say we should act on principle, following reason.

You can work to bring about change in the world, but you won't make much difference. In a short time, people will forget about you and what you did. All the truths you defend have been refuted already and will be refuted again. Ideas bury those who argue about them. There's just the endless repetition of reasons and seasons, of life and death.

There's nothing to get excited about. You're never going to discover or create something really new. Just face it — *there's nothing new under the sun.*

There are no new truths, but only truths that have not been recognized by those who have perceived them without noticing.
Mary McCarthy
On the Contrary

IT'S TRUE THAT most of what can be said about reality and about morality has been said. There doesn't seem to have been any particular advance in human understanding since the ancients. We still experience triumph and defeat; we still live for our short time on earth, die, and are forgotten. But if it's true that there's nothing new, how is it that you discovered this?

What is it for you to know something, anyway? Think about a difficult problem that you struggled with and eventually came to understand. The fact that your teacher understood it didn't mean you did. Learning isn't just automatic. Every piece of knowledge learned by every human being is a brand new event.

Each one of us is a unique, living center of intelligence and freedom. Think about what it is to be conscious. Is your consciousness mine or somebody else's? No, it's yours alone, and it's new every moment. What about free choices? Can a free choice be just a repetition? If it were, it wouldn't be free. So every thought and choice of every person is a new event.

Not just human beings, but every living thing is constantly being renewed. To be alive is to be a center of independent activity, which isn't reducible to the environment. Even the inanimate world transcends mere repetition. The universe is expanding, and the gravitational relations between things are ever different. Nothing, then, is really just the recycled past.

Although there's continuity and repetition in everything under the sun, each act of under-standing, every choice and heartbeat — even every beam of sunlight — is new.

Nothing is repeated,
and everything
is unparalleled.
Edmond and Jules de Goncourt
Journal

Things just
look different

Of course, things appear to be different,
but don't be fooled by appearances. Deep
down, everything's the same. The bottom
line is that it's all just matter and energy.

Progress in modern science has demonstrated the truth of
this fact. Everything we see and experience is ultimately
made up of the same stuff. Rocks, flowers, animals, and
people are all composed of material particles moving about
according to forces of energy. Ultimately, matter and energy
are the same, too: break up matter, and you get energy.

Understand this, and you'll have the key to understanding
all things. Any question whatever — about the stars or the
planets, about the life of bugs, even about the choices of
human beings — can be answered by reference to these
universal principles. No, it's not simple, and we're not there
yet; but in the end, it's just interactions of matter and energy.

Don't be duped by your senses. On the surface, things don't seem to be the same. But
analyze them: you'll find they're all made of
the same stuff — *things just look different.*

*The nature of everything is dual — matter and void; or particles
and space, wherein the former move about. Except for void
and substance, nothing, no third alternative, no other
nature can possibly exist in the sum of things.*
Lucretius
Nature of Things, Bk. 1

I T'S TRUE THAT all things are interrelated: that's why we call it a universe (instead of a multiverse). And everything we see and experience is composed of the same basic particles, which move in accordance with the fundamental forces that physics has discovered. But if we see things only in terms of their common elements, are we in danger of failing to see them at all?

Granted, human beings, animals, plants, rocks, molecules, and atoms have something in common. But can what's common explain why they're distinct? Can rocks explain plants, or plants explain animals, or animals explain human beings? Are matter, life, sensation, and freedom all really the same thing?

When we explain what something is, we try to pinpoint its characteristic unity. There's the unity that is the human being, the unity that is the frog, the unity that is the rose, the piece of granite, the molecule, the atom. When you analyze something into its parts, you explain it by some lesser unity. You ignore its particular unity, and don't explain it: you explain it away.

Break down water into oxygen and hydrogen, and you no longer have water. Shoot an elephant, and you no longer have an elephant. Consider Mary as merely an animal, or alive, or chemically complex, or a bunch of atoms, and you've missed her distinct intelligence, freedom, and humor. You've failed to see the unique self that shines through her eyes and her smile.

Although things have much in common, what they have in common can't explain how they're unique. Things don't just look different: they really are different.

Natural things seem to be arranged in degrees. Mixed things are more perfect than elements, and plants than minerals, animals than plants, and men than other animals. The universe would not be perfect if only one grade of goodness were found in things.
St. Thomas Aquinas
Summa Theologica I, 47, 2

Think for yourself

It's no good just going along with what you're taught. You're a unique individual; your situation is unlike anybody else's. You've got to take charge of your life.

In order to really learn, you have to think for yourself. You can't learn math by just memorizing formulas: you've got to understand the equations. You can't judge an idea to be true or false unless you compare it with ideas and evidence that you understand. You can't make good ethical decisions unless you understand why some things are right and others wrong.

To be creative or inventive, you've got to do your own thinking. Who cares what others have said? The important thing is to find a way to be original. You've got to come up with an angle that hasn't been thought of before. If you don't, you'll just be one more cog in the machine. What a bore to live in a world of thoughtless conformity. Make a difference!

You've got to think for yourself to understand anything. And, if you're going to make a mark in the world, you've got to be independent and creative. *Think for yourself!*

Most people are other people. Their thoughts are someone else's opinions, their lives a mimicry, their passions a quotation.
Oscar Wilde
De Profundis

I T'S TRUE THAT learning is not just memorizing what others tell you; you've got to understand it and then judge its truth. Learning is activity, not just passive indoctrination. And the only way for you to be really original is to free yourself from routine patterns of thought. But without some dependence on others, can your thought bear any fruit whatsoever?

Imagine if everyone had only original thoughts. Many ideas would be bizarre, indecipherable to others, perhaps incomprehensible in themselves, and certainly not a reflection of reality. There would be no common language and could be no progress in thought. Independence like that is worthless, even dangerous.

Fruitful originality is built upon the thoughts and discoveries of others. It's impossible to imagine today's progress in physics apart from the work of Einstein. Breakthroughs in medicine are built on years of research. Without Mozart, Beethoven's brilliance might never have flowered. Shakespeare builds on a tradition from Homer and Sophocles to Dante and Chaucer.

Thinking for yourself can't mean starting from scratch. Far from being independent and free, you'd be forced to reinvent the wheel before you could get rolling. Reliance on others frees you from much routine work. More importantly, others can teach you a lot about the creative process. Following their lead, you can learn to bring your unique insights to fruition.

> *Only you can do your own thinking, but don't fail to help yourself to what others have thought. Their discoveries and example will help you think better when you think for yourself.*

Thinking in isolation and with pride ends in being an idiot.
G. K. Chesterton
Orthodoxy, Ch. III

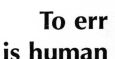

To err
is human

We all make mistakes. It's part of
being human. You can't expect people
always to be good. It's just not natural.
We can't be perfect; give people a break!

Nobody's right all of the time. Even the best mathematicians
had to be corrected somewhere along the way. Look at all
the scientific conclusions that have turned out to be mistaken.
Who among us never forgets someone's name, or where we
put something, or what we were supposed to get at the store?
It's impossible to be right all of the time. No one can do it.

The same holds true for ethical mistakes. We all fail to think
about others as much as we should. And even when we think
about them, we don't always follow through on helping them.
Who's never been envious, greedy, or angry? Who's never
lied? We all have. Sure, we should try to be good, but we've
got to be realistic. Admit it. We all mess up sometimes.

It's impossible to be perfect, whether
we're talking about knowledge, action, or
morality. To expect perfection is to expect
too much. Lighten up. *To err is human.*

*I cling to my imperfection, as
the very essence of my being.*
Anatole France
The Garden of Epicurus

I T'S TRUE THAT we all make mistakes. As what we learn in school becomes more complicated, we inevitably get some things wrong. Our memories aren't perfect, nor are any of us free from moral failure. Clearly, we all fail in one way or another. But is making mistakes inevitable? Is it as much a part of being human as living, sensing, and thinking?

Do we know what things are by noting their defects? Do we know what a washing machine is by noting that it doesn't clean clothes? Or a cucumber seed by noting that it fails to produce a plant and fruit? Do we know what human nature is by noting that we make mistakes? Isn't it just the opposite?

Don't we have to know what something's supposed to be, before we can see its defects? The washing machine ought to clean clothes. The cucumber seed ought to produce a plant and fruit. Likewise, human beings are meant to know the truth and choose the good. Only by knowing this can we see that we'd be better off if we didn't make mistakes or choose what's evil.

We can see, then, that humans are meant to know, not to err, even though experience teaches us that we all do, in fact, err. It's certainly not inevitable that we'll be wise and good; but there's no reason why we can't be, either. There's nothing in our nature that makes it impossible. To be human is to be made for perfection, and to be fully human is to strive for it.

> *Although all of us do, in fact, fail to know*
> *and act perfectly, we're not made for such*
> *failure. In our experience, to be human is*
> *to err, but to err is not what makes us human.*

Every soul that strives to love and desire supreme happiness will at some point enjoy it.
St. Anselm
Monologion, 70

Trust
your feelings

Anything that feels so good just can't
be wrong. We're made to be happy
and feel pleasure. It's our nature. So
believe your feelings — they never lie.

Human beings are sensitive animals. Our instincts are the
product of thousands of years of evolution. Our physical and
emotional sensitivity evolved to guide us. Beyond the instincts
of the other animals, we've developed a kind of instinct to be
good, a moral sense. It's a universal feeling that we all have
for other human beings, a kind of natural benevolence.

Some claim that we should put our trust in reason. But reason
is a relative newcomer in our evolutionary development. It's
really only suited to manipulating facts and figures. Applied
to moral issues, it's always inconclusive: there's always an
argument that can be made supporting the other side. In
the end, it's feelings that move us to action, not reason.

So don't get trapped in the endless debate
about morality. Be honest: it's not reason
that guides us, but something much more
reliable. When in doubt, *trust your feelings*.

Morality, therefore, is more properly felt than judged of.
To have the sense of virtue is nothing but to feel a satis-
faction of a particular kind. The very feeling constitutes
our praise or admiration. We go no farther.
David Hume
An Enquiry Concerning the Principles of Morals, IX

I T'S TRUE THAT feelings and emotions are fundamental to our humanity. We're creatures guided, at least in part, by instincts and reactions to pleasure and pain. Many of the bonds of friendship and community arise from a kind of natural empathy. It's obvious that we should nurture such feelings. But if we think we should, aren't we trusting in something besides feelings?

Granted that we have some natural benevolence for each other, we also sometimes feel angry, or jealous, or afraid. If we have contradictory feelings, how do we know which one to trust? What tells us that we ought to be kind instead of violent or manipulative? Why follow one feeling rather than another?

Not only do we have many different feelings, but our feelings are notoriously changeable. Think of your feelings toward someone you love — your mother, child, spouse, or friend. Hardly a day goes by without your feelings of love changing to anger, frustration, or disappointment. Should you just follow these feelings? Shouldn't you try to guide them back to love?

What about other people following their feelings, in particular when they're not in your favor? Would you approve of their mistreating you if they felt like it? On the contrary, you expect them to do the right thing by you, to think intelligently, to control their bad feelings, and to encourage good feelings toward you. This is the work of reason, not feeling — a matter of choice, not impulse.

Feelings often do guide us, and sometimes guide us well. But they can't justify their preferences. Don't just trust your feelings; let reason guide your feelings, and feel good about it.

We may have feelings of fear, courage, desire, anger, pity, and pleasure or pain more or less than we should. But to have these feelings at the right times, for the right things, toward the right men, for the right purpose, and in the right manner is virtue.
Aristotle
Nicomachean Ethics, II, 6

Truth's a matter of perspective

No one has a God's-eye view of things. Every judgment is from one particular perspective. Truth is always relative to the individual and the situation.

It's like sitting in a circle with others, looking at a sculpture of a man in the middle. No two see exactly the same thing. One sees the face; another sees the back of the head. Even those sitting close to each other don't see quite the same thing. I see the nose from the front, the person next to me sees it from an angle. It's the same with knowing the truth about things.

This is even more obvious in moral judgments. People come from different backgrounds, they've had different experiences, and they find themselves in unique situations. No two people or situations are exactly the same. You see things differently depending on whether you're male or female, rich or poor, threatened or secure. It all depends on your perspective.

Let's be honest. We're all limited in our knowledge. Nobody can see things from all sides at once. Whether we like it or not, *truth's a matter of perspective.*

Some wonder that disputes about opinions should so often end in personalities; but such disputes begin with personalities; for our opinions are a part of ourselves. After the first contradiction, it is ourselves, and not the thing, we maintain.
Edward Fitzgerald
Polonius

I T'S TRUE THAT we all see things from slightly different points of view. This is literally true for sense experience, but also true for understanding and moral judgments. We bring to our insights personal strengths and weaknesses, and a unique sum of experiences. But if all truth's a matter of perspective, what's the point of trying to get me to see things your way?

How can you get me to see what you mean if our perspectives are decisively different? If it's all a matter of perspective, then your statement "truth's a matter of perspective" is itself just a matter of perspective. So why should I bother to take it seriously? Even if I want to understand you, apparently I can't.

If we're to have meaningful conversations with each other, then the differences between the way we think can't be more basic than the similarities. We don't have a hard time accepting this for mathematical thought. Perspectives are irrelevant to understanding the equation "2+2=4". Nor does anybody think that the laws of gravity differ according to perspective.

It's when we consider moral judgments that perspective seems more decisive. Values are harder to judge than numbers and facts. However, if moral truth is a matter of perspective, then no judgment of injustice is certain. But we rightly refuse to accept the murderer's perspective as the criterion for moral truth. We are certain that deliberately killing innocent people is wrong.

> *It's true that there are many legitimate per-spectives, but only because truth is not merely a matter of perspective. The right perspective on truth is that it can and should be found.*

I know that seven plus three equals ten, not just now, but always; it never has been and never will be the case that seven plus three does not equal ten. This incorruptible truth of number is common to me and all who think.
St. Augustine
On Free Choice of the Will, Bk. 2, Ch. 8

Violence never solved anything

Violence isn't the answer. All it does is hurt people and make them thirsty for revenge. Nonviolence is the only good response to violence.

Look at the problems in Northern Ireland and the Middle East. The violence of the IRA just intensifies the resolve of the Protestants not to let the IRA have its way. The same is true in Israel. The terrorism of the suicide bombers infuriates the Israelis. The retaliations by the Israelis galvanize anti-Israeli sentiment among the Palestinians. It's an endless cycle.

People never forget pain and oppression. The argument that your violence is merely retribution for theirs simply doesn't work. People only remember the last outrage. The only solution is to break this cycle of revenge. Pride must yield to conciliation. Either there's got to be a negotiated settlement, or someone's got to give in. Otherwise, violence will never end.

Don't let your emotions run away with you. Use your mind. Ask yourself what's the best way to bring peace. Don't strike back. *Violence never solved anything.*

History never lies! Justice seemingly gained through the use of violence only begets more violence and oppression.
John Bryson Chane
Episcopal Bishop

I T'S TRUE THAT violence often leads to more violence. We tend
to remember the harm done to us more than the harm we've
inflicted on others. We feel unjustly treated. So does the other
side. Violence is never a sufficient answer. You've got to get to
the root of the problem. Still, wasn't your right to espouse nonviolence without getting persecuted won for you by violence?

Would Nazi Germany or Japan have given up their plans for
world domination if not forced to? Tyrants consume the rights of
their subjects; and some tyrants think that all people should be
their subjects. If not for the violent defeat of aggression in the
past, you wouldn't be free to voice your opinion today.

Violence isn't always the right response to violent injustice,
nor should it ever be the whole response. If the injustice can be
thwarted by peaceful means, then violence isn't justified. And
even if violence is justified, it should be directed to justice and
peace. The injustice should be stopped and friendship between
the parties promoted, as was the case with the Marshall Plan.

But nonviolence can't be the whole response either. It may,
in fact, encourage more violence in the long run. If you let someone get away with injustice, you encourage that person to be
more unjust. Everyone agrees that the policy of appeasing Hitler
in the early stages of WWII was imprudent. Defeating him
earlier would have saved many lives on both sides.

Since violence has defeated evil tyrants,
violence has solved some things. But alone,
violence can't bring justice and peace, for
violence never solves everything.

If all young people in America were to act as you
intend to act, the country would be defenseless
and easily delivered into slavery.
Albert Einstein
Letter to a pacifist, 1941

What is
truth?

How can you claim to know the truth?
There's just so much to know, and it's
all so complicated. What was thought to
be true yesterday is proven false today.

Even today's experts don't agree. Say you want to know
why people act the way they do. If you ask a professor of
philosophy, you'll hear about free choices and virtues. Ask a
psychologist, and you'll hear all about needs, desires, and
personality traits; or maybe he'll tell you about the influences
of upbringing and social conditioning on our actions.

But that's not the end of the disagreement. A biologist will
explain human action in terms of environment, life force, and
the functions of organs. A chemist will deny the adequacy of
that explanation: he'll say it really comes down to chemical
combinations. That doesn't go far enough, says the physicist:
really, everything is just matter and energy. Who's right?

It's clear there's no such thing as truth.
What's considered true is relative to time,
place, and perspective. *What is truth?*
No one can say for certain.

*Protagoras says that in Nature nothing exists
but doubt: that everything is equally open to
discussion, including the assertion that
everything is equally open to discussion.*
Michel de Montaigne
An Apology for Raymond Sebond

I T'S TRUE THAT knowing the truth is not easy. Reality is complex. New discoveries make obsolete today what was thought to be true yesterday. Widespread disagreement about what's true certainly challenges the idea of universal truth. Competing explanatory theories by the experts seem to be irreconcilable. Still, can it really be true that there is no truth?

Can you honestly doubt the truth that you exist? You know you can't because you have to exist to be able to doubt. Do you doubt you are reading this sentence? That would be silly. And what about "2+2=4"? What reason can you possibly give for doubting this and other simple mathematical truths?

You know these things immediately through sense experience and reflection. You don't need some highly trained specialist to show you. You're an expert on this stuff just because you're a rational human being. And even when you try to deny these truths, you have to rely on other truths. When you say "there is no truth," you're claiming that your statement is true.

In fact, it's impossible to make any judgment at all without presuming that there is truth. Of course, discovering the truth in a particular area may be difficult. We have to make sure we're aware of all the relevant facts. We must strive to keep long and intricate arguments in focus. But even to claim that these difficulties are real is itself to insist on some truth.

So what is truth? That depends on what the topic is. And some truths we may never know. But that truth exists is absolutely certain. It can't be true that there is no truth.

Even if I'm in error, I am undoubtedly not in error about knowing that I exist. It follows that I'm not in error about knowing that I know. When I delight in these two things, I add a third thing that is equal to them.
St. Augustine
City of God, Bk. 11, Ch. 26

What's done
is done

You can't change the past. Whatever has happened is now fixed forever. Not even God can undo what's gone before. You've just got to face the facts, and move on.

The past is dead and gone. All those "what-might-have-beens" are irretrievably lost. You know that it's impossible to go back and undo the things you've done. So why worry about it? There's no sense in crying over spilt milk. It just won't help at all. No amount of tears will ever get the milk back in the cup; no amount of regret will cause the past to change.

So don't carry the burden of the past on your shoulders. All you'll end up doing is ruining the present for yourself and for those around you. Just forget about what's happened and focus on the future. Nations and cultures, too, have to move on. The problems of the past are part of a history that just can't be changed. We've got to let bygones be bygones.

There's nothing you can do about the past. Time is a one-way street: you can't turn back. The future is free; look to the future and forget the past. *What's done is done.*

Things without remedy should be without regret: what's done is done.
William Shakespeare
Macbeth, Act 3, Sc. 2

I T'S TRUE THAT the course of past events can't be changed. There's no way to go back in time and undo the bad things you wish you hadn't done or to do the good deeds you wish you had done. Dwelling on what might have been can lead to frustration and despair, and the future is free and all before us. But is it desirable or even possible to have done with the past?

It doesn't seem possible to cut ourselves off from the past. Our very sanity is a consciousness of our continuity with the past. It's the mark of the insane that they cannot connect events in an orderly way. We cannot imagine a future coming to be without remembering how events unfolded in the past.

The characters of individuals and institutions are at any moment the products of the past. Our moral characters have been formed by the choices we've made. Our institutions — families, schools, colleges, and government — have been formed by cooperation in choices and actions. We're free to make new choices, which sustain or modify our past choices.

So to the extent that it lives on in our characters and institutions, the past is not fixed. What's done can, in some sense, be undone. We can reform our characters. We can apologize for our faults and heal damaged friendships. We can correct and improve the living traditions that are our institutions; we can change practices and overturn bad laws.

What's done cannot be undone by turning back the clock. But much of the wrong we've done can be transformed by our freely remembering and correcting past choices.

For a conscious being, to exist is to change, to change is to mature, to mature is to go on creating oneself endlessly.
Henri Bergson
Creative Evolution

Whatever
makes you happy

Happiness is just a matter of personal preference. There's no such thing as one kind of happiness for everybody, so we should just do what makes us happy.

What makes people happy? Look around. Some people are happy studying. They like it so much, they want to go to college. Others would rather work at McDonald's and buy a car. Some like to play sports. Some want to join the theater group. Others just want to hang out. As long as you're not hurting anybody, it doesn't matter what you do.

You know what? It's actually good that the same things don't make us happy. If they did, we'd all want to do the same thing, and then what would happen to society? To have a lively community, we've got to have different interests. Some people have to be businessmen, some teach school, some be doctors, some entertain, and some just be consumers.

Why worry about fulfilling some ideal? I may not be a big success, much of a brain, or a great helper of mankind, but I'm happy. Be like me. *Do whatever makes you happy.*

To enjoy yourself and make others enjoy themselves, without harming yourself or others; that, to my mind, is the whole of ethics.
Sébastien Chamfort
Maximes et Pensées

I T'S TRUE THAT we all want to be happy and that we pursue a variety of goals and occupations to make us happy. We don't have the same talents or interests. Nor should we. It's clearly good for society that people pursue their different vocations. But if happiness is something we all pursue, isn't there something universal and objective about it?

No doubt, there are many things that contribute to our happiness. We need external goods to keep us alive. We enjoy pleasure and hate pain. We like to know what's what and to exercise our free will to shape our lives. But as good as these things are, are they of equal importance in our happiness?

How important to our happiness are external goods? We don't desire money and possessions for their own sakes, but for what they can do for us. They allow us to live, to find pleasure in what we enjoy, and to help our friends. We *have* external goods; but we *want* to be happy. We choose external goods to help us attain happiness, so they can't be the core of happiness.

Closer to the heart of happiness are the things we desire for their own sakes: things like pleasure, truth, and virtue. Pleasure, however, is fleeting, and we want happiness to last. If it is to last, happiness must lie in things not easily taken away, nor easily lost. Unlike pleasure, truth and virtue are not fleeting. No one can take them away from you. They are long-lasting.

> *By all means, pursue what makes you happy.*
> *But when you do, don't settle for whatever*
> *happens. Insist on the only real happiness —*
> *happiness you can know, cherish, and keep.*

Are you not ashamed of your eagerness to possess as much wealth, reputation and honors as possible, while you do not care for wisdom or truth, or the state of your soul?
Plato
Apology, 29e

Whatever will be, will be

You don't know what tomorrow will bring. Anyway, there's little you can do about it. So why worry about the future? Resign yourself to the inevitable.

What good will it do to fret over what college you'll get into, or what kind of job you'll find? There are so many unknowns that it's impossible for us to piece the future together. What's impossible is not worth trying. You'll just end up making yourself miserable now. Let tomorrow take care of itself. You've got enough to do to get through today.

This is not being pessimistic; it's just being realistic. You're not master of the future, so you might as well admit it. Optimism is fine in its place, but it's no substitute for truth. Face things as they are now, and leave the future to fate. This is real wisdom — to keep focused on what you have now. And this is real courage — to face the future without expectations.

So don't get caught up in hopes or fears about tomorrow. The future's beyond your control. What's here right now is real. And *whatever will be, will be.*

*Let me get through today, and
I shall not fear tomorrow.*
St. Philip Neri

IT'S TRUE THAT we're ignorant of what the future holds. Many factors beyond our control make it impossible to determine what's in store for us. To worry about what we can't change is useless. We must admit our limitations. But isn't the decision whether or not to resign yourself to the future a choice within your power to make, and won't this choice affect the future?

Although we're not masters of the future, are we slaves to fate? Truly, there are many factors beyond our control that will influence the future, from the operations of physical forces to the choices of others. But some choices are clearly ours, including choosing how to accept what we can't change.

Although it's true that the future will be the way it will be, the future is not yet. It has not been fixed so that our choices are futile. The shape of the future depends in part on our free choices. Whether or not I work hard in school makes a big difference in where I go to college. The effort I put into my friendship contributes to the future success of that friendship.

Of course, the future is not just up to us. We don't control the physical world or the choices of others. But even if we can't know what the future will bring — what bad things may happen, how other people will treat us — we can know that patience, love, and generosity will grow, at least somewhere. That is, they'll grow in our actions if we decide that they should.

There may not be much we can do to change the course of world history, but we can ensure through our choices that whatever will be, will be at least a little bit better.

*I do not believe in a fate that falls on men however they act;
I do believe in a fate that falls on them unless they act.*
G. K. Chesterton
Generally Speaking, Ch. 20

When in Rome, do as the Romans do

We've got to get along. It's no good being rude. When you enter someone else's world, don't insult the way she lives. Don't make waves; find a way to fit in.

If you visit someone's home, don't criticize her manners or the way she decorates her living room. Just because she does things differently from what you're used to doesn't mean she's wrong. You don't have the right to judge her. Why should she do things the way you would? How do you know it's better, anyway? Just be polite and show respect for your hostess.

The same thing's true with cultural and moral differences. Not everyone thinks the same things are important. If you find yourself in a foreign cultural or strange moral context, be tolerant and accept those around you. Besides, if you're open and pay attention, you may learn something new and valuable. Trying to fit in is both polite and instructive.

There's no best way of doing things. Each culture has its rules. Don't be so ignorant and arrogant as to think you know best. *When in Rome, do as the Romans do.*

When you are at Rome, live in the Roman style; if you are elsewhere, live as they live elsewhere.
Jeremy Taylor
Ductor Dubitantium, Bk. 1, Ch. 1

IT'S TRUE THAT we should be courteous to those we visit. We should make every effort to get along. We can show good will by adopting the customs of the host family or nation. Such good will and ready compliance brings trust and mutual understanding. But what should you do if your hosts deny that people should try to adapt to their moral surroundings?

Suppose they think that there are universal moral norms that we all should follow. If you're convinced that you should accept the opinions of your hosts, what do you do? Do you give up your relativism? Or what if they think that people like you should be enslaved? Do you let yourself be enslaved? Of course not.

If adapting your behavior to your surroundings involves morally indifferent things, such as the way you cut your hair, the clothes you wear, or your table manners, then there's nothing wrong with adapting. In fact, it might be something you really ought to do. After all, we should do what we can to spread friendship and mutual understanding wherever we go.

But if your willingness to adapt involves serious moral matters, it's a different story. Moral principles are not based on what people prefer. Some acts are always and everywhere wrong, like cheating in business, abusing children, or murdering the innocent. So what if those around you do them? You shouldn't join in — not even to fit in or make them comfortable.

> *As long as the Romans are doing good (or at least neutral) things, by all means, do as they do. But when their actions are evil, do as good people — not as the Romans — do.*

We achieve universal tolerance when we respect what's characteristic in nations, clinging, though, to the conviction that the truly meritorious belongs to all mankind.
Johann Wolfgang von Goethe
Letter to Thomas Carlyle, 8/20/1827

Who's to judge?

Different cultures have different morals.
Even in the same culture people have
different values. Who are you to say that
yours are better than anyone else's?

Just because you were raised to think and act in a certain way
doesn't give you the right to sit in judgment over people who
think and act differently — or (worse yet) to impose your personal values on them. They probably think your beliefs and
actions are wrong, too. You don't want them to force you to
change your ways, so don't try to force them to change theirs.

Anyway, you can never know what a person is going through
in life. You can't judge actions without taking into account
circumstances. The poor steal because they have to eat.
People suffering traumatic pain want to die because they
can't bear any more pain. These are personal choices that
only someone in the same situation can fully appreciate.

Let people decide for themselves. You're not
God; you don't understand all cultures or every
circumstance. Why do you think *you* know
what's right and wrong? *Who's to judge?*

Normality is culturally defined. We recognize
that morality differs in every society, and
is a convenient term for socially
approved habits.
Ruth Benedict
"Anthropology and the Abnormal"

I T'S TRUE THAT differences in circumstances, upbringing, and culture create diverse opinions about values. It can be hard to say who's right and who's wrong. And legitimate differences in tastes, dress, and customs deserve respect. But if morality depends completely on circumstances, upbringing, and culture, can any action ever be wrong . . . or right?

After all, no two people have exactly the same upbringing, nor are circumstances ever exactly the same for different people or even for the same person at different times. So if background and circumstances are decisive, no act is really right or wrong; and no choice can ever be worthy of praise or blame.

But if a stranger came up to you on the street and shot you, you'd judge it to be wrong. You wouldn't care if his culture or family had taught him that it was fine to shoot innocent people. Or if someone raped your sister, you wouldn't excuse him because, in the circumstances, he felt like doing it. You would judge these actions to be wrong, and you'd be right to do so.

It's true that many cases are unclear and hard to judge, due to complicated facts or uncertain motives. However, others, like the ones mentioned above, are clearly wrong. In these clear cases, you easily make judgments, and you can make others, too. When you do, you rely on knowledge of standards that apply in all circumstances and that hold for you and everyone else.

> So who's to judge? You and I are; and so are
> "nonjudgmental" people. In clear cases, we
> all can and should make moral judgments.
> Let's learn to make good ones.

Consider the following: one ought to live justly; everyone should be given what's rightly his. Don't you agree that these are true, and that they are present in common to me and you and all who see them?
St. Augustine
On Free Choice of the Will, Bk. 2

Why trust
reason, anyway?

We're always told to be reasonable, but why should we? How do I know that reason isn't just a big blunder? Give me one good reason I should trust reason.

There are lots of reasons to doubt reason. We've been wrong so many times before. We've been wrong about the nature of reality. Ptolemy looks foolish next to Newton; Newton looks foolish next to Einstein. We've been wrong about morality, too. We used to think that slavery was right; now we know it's wrong. Women weren't allowed to vote; now they are.

To argue for reason is to assume what you're trying to prove. That's the biggest fallacy in the book. After all, the only way you can convince me that reason is worth using is to use reason. But if reason is flawed, then even though I think that you give me grounds for agreeing with you, we could both be wrong. Maybe logical certainty is just an elaborate deception.

There's no way we can be certain that our conclusions are correct. Too many people have claimed to know the truth and been wrong. *Why trust reason, anyway?*

What peculiar privilege has this little agitation of the brain which we call "thought," that we must thus make it a model for the whole universe?
David Hume
Dialogues Concerning Natural Religion, Part II

I T'S TRUE THAT we don't have some absolute guarantee that reason works. We have no deductive proof that reason is reliable. And, of course, we have made mistakes in the past. It seems impossible to be sure that we're not making a mistake right now. Even if we think we are certain, we could be wrong. But isn't it contradictory to argue that reason is defective?

How can you argue for anything at all if reason is flawed? More precisely, how can you believe your argument is worth anything if you don't believe reason works? It's simply contradictory to present reasons for doubting reason, to try to prove that proof is impossible, to argue that all arguments fail.

It's clear that the starting point in every chain of reasoning can't be proven. If everything must be proven, then nothing can be proven. But what kind of starting point is legitimate? You can't just assume anything you like. The only thing that can be both certain and unproven is what's self-evident. This is where we must start — with those things that are too obvious to doubt.

You can tell if it's too obvious to doubt because, when you try to doubt it, you end up contradicting yourself. If you doubt reason and try to prove your case, you are trusting the very reason your argument seeks to discredit. And if you fall silent in order not to contradict yourself, you betray the fact that you see reason works. The power of reason is too obvious to doubt.

Although it's reasonable to revisit the conclusions of reason in light of new evidence, it's unreasonable to doubt reason itself. There is no good reason to refuse to trust reason.

If the value of our reasoning is in doubt, you cannot try to establish it by reasoning. Reason is our starting point. There can be no question either of attacking or defending it.
C. S. Lewis
Miracles, Ch. 3

You can only love others as much as you love yourself

It's impossible to love others if you hate yourself. So get yourself together; then you can help others. If you don't, you'll just make a mess of others and yourself.

People who are unhappy with themselves can't possibly make other people happy. Consider the overbearing mother who spends all her time and energy on her children. She thinks she's loving them, but she's making their lives miserable. Or consider the person who helps others because of guilt over his own inadequacies. His help lacks any real root in love.

It's partly a function of time. If you spend all your time trying to care for others, there simply won't be any to appreciate your own worth and develop your potential. How can you really know who you are if you don't stop to think about it? Take some time out to be alone and to meet your own needs. Then you'll be ready for the task of helping others.

First things first. Only if you're happy with who you are will you be able to make others happy. It's as simple as that. *You can only love others as much as you love yourself.*

How can we expect charity toward others, when we are uncharitable toward ourselves?
Sir Thomas Browne
Religio Medici

I T'S TRUE THAT self-loathing does nobody any good. It's always debilitating for you, and your outward acts of generosity will never compensate for a feeling of failure. Your heart won't be in it, and this will show. You need a genuine source of love within you. Hypocrisy is deadly for all human relations. But is it even possible to love yourself without loving others first?

What does love mean, anyway? Without a doubt, we all want to be loved. Does this mean that we want others to love themselves or us? Clearly, we want them to love us. If they don't, they're not loving at all. Isn't the same thing true for us? If we love at all, don't we have to put the one we love first?

In a way, of course, it's natural to put ourselves first. As animals, we're instinctually programmed to survive in a hostile environment. We have certain needs, like food and shelter, that must be met, or we die. Clearly, we have to preserve our own lives if we're going to be of any use to others. Putting ourselves first is understandable, but it's not worthy of love.

Along with our instincts, we have intelligence and free will. Through intelligence, we can put ourselves in another's shoes. Through free will, we can choose to ignore our own desires for the sake of helping someone else. Love is caring for another for that other's own sake, not for what we get out of it. Love others. Then, since love is good, you'll be worthy of love.

Loving yourself and loving others are related. But rather than your love for others depending on loving yourself, you can only love yourself as much as you love others.

Children are taught to respect certain people. By giving respect, they hope to gain self-respect, and through self-respect, they gain the respect of others.
Henry Old Coyote
U.S. Educator

You can't argue with success

You want to know who to listen to? Those who have been successful. They know what they're talking about because they've been there and done that.

You've got to admit they're doing something right. People don't get to the top unless they've got real talent. Look at the fruits of their labor — the money, the prestige, the glamour. You criticize their lifestyles and choices. But you know what? You're just envious. They've made it and you haven't. You can't do what they've done, so you say it's not worth doing.

Maybe you think they don't deserve their success or that what they're doing isn't important. Maybe you think they get paid too much and receive too much praise. Or maybe you question how they get to the top. You say they're just lucky or their methods are questionable, but what difference does it make? Success shows that they know how to get things done.

We're a society that honors individual initiative. To those who make it, we give fame and material rewards. That's the way it should be. *You can't argue with success.*

Money is indeed the most important thing in the world; and all sound and successful personal and national morality should have this fact for its basis.
George Bernard Shaw
The Irrational Knot, Preface

IT'S TRUE THAT those who are successful deserve recognition. Success is usually a sign of real commitment and dedication. Enterprise should be encouraged; hard work and creativity are good. And we have to guard against envy. We must never deny the value of someone's accomplishments just because they're not ours. But what is it really to be successful?

Power, money, and fame are the most common measures of success. But are they the most important ones? Does money indicate the true value of what people do? Is fame a reliable judge of success? What if the power, money, and fame come from luck or from doing something morally wrong?

A successful player of the lottery is lucky but deserves no praise. He didn't do anything good to deserve the money. In fact, gambling seems closer to vice than virtue. And does the rich and famous professional athlete or rock star lead a life more valuable and praiseworthy than the social worker or dedicated teacher whom no one's heard of and who's paid one tenth as much?

If money and fame were praiseworthy in themselves, then the clever swindler and the famously cruel tyrant would deserve our praise. But morally bad choices are not praiseworthy in themselves, nor are they validated by the power, money, or fame that they bring. In fact, it is good choices — those that are just, honest, kind, and wise — that we praise most of all.

> You can't argue with success that's based on honest work and talent. But you can and should argue about what true success is and what methods of achieving it are acceptable.

A day spent without the sight or sound of beauty, the contemplation of mystery, or the search for truth and perfection is a poverty-stricken day; and a succession of such days is fatal to human life.
Lewis Mumford
The Condition of Man

You can't stand in the way of progress

Who can turn back the tide? Change is inevitable, so you might as well accept it. Either get on the train of progress or get run over.

Look what happens to people who try to resist change. They're soon forgotten or mocked as reactionaries. Think of those who opposed Galileo, how silly they were to cling to their outmoded ideas. And those who opposed Darwin are discredited today. Science has proven that all life — including human life — has evolved. All aspects of our lives fit this progressive model.

Admit it. In the last few centuries, progress in science and technology has benefited our lives tremendously. With each generation, medical advances improve our health. Today, we can travel around the earth in hours. We communicate with anyone in the world. Even our ethics have progressed: some things right in the past are wrong now, and vice versa.

Progress is inevitable, so you might as well be part of it. Many good things are still to be discovered. Get on board. *You can't stand in the way of progress.*

The progress of the human race must be considered susceptible of modification only with regard to its speed, and without any reversal in the order of development.
Auguste Comte
Positive Philosophy, VI, 3

I'T'S TRUE THAT some change is inevitable and that, over the last few centuries, changes in science and technology have been rapid and productive. We've seen great progress in our knowledge of the physical world, in fighting disease, and in our ability to communicate. But if we find things progressing in the wrong direction, shouldn't we stand in their way?

If I do, I may wind up in trouble. But should I always avoid trouble? If the direction of change is clearly good, then standing in the way of it is wrong. But not all progressions are equally good. Has our "progress" in wisdom and justice matched our glorious progress in science and technology?

A quick look at the 20th century, with its wars and oppressive regimes, makes it clear that there's no inevitability in our progress toward universal peace and human rights. More people were killed in wars of the last century than in all other wars combined. Is such a progression of violence inevitable? Can't we (and shouldn't we) stand in the way of such progress?

Neither are the changes in morality through the last fifty years obvious improvements. Look at the growing focus on self-interest and greed in many businesses and in our personal lives. Although we seem to be growing progressively less interested in helping others, it surely does not follow that such progress is inevitable or that it should be accepted.

Things change, but not all change is good. When we find that changes are progressing toward what's worse, we can and should stand in the way of such "progress."

Progress, properly understood, has indeed a most dignified and legitimate meaning. But as used in opposition to precise moral ideals, it is ludicrous.
G. K. Chesterton
Heretics

You scratch my back, and I'll scratch yours

Here's how we get along: whatever you do for me, I'll do for you. This is the basis for all morality. It keeps us out of trouble and gives us the help we need.

There's a built-in reciprocity here that makes things fair. If you help me build my house, I'll help with yours. If you come to my aid when I'm in trouble, I'll come to yours when you need me. Neither party has to do more than the other. We both know what's expected of us. Such reciprocity is the basis for community. We cooperate with each other on clear terms.

If we all followed this rule, the world would be in excellent shape. You could initiate some act of generosity and expect the same thing would be done for you. It's really just another version of the golden rule: do unto others what you would have them do unto you. Both individuals and the community stand to benefit. The results are good for you and good for me.

Help me, and I'll help you. Defend my interests, and I'll defend yours. It's the way of the world. *You scratch my back, and I'll scratch yours.*

The principle of self-interest is not a lofty one, but it is clear and sure. It checks one personal interest by another, and uses, to direct the passions, the very same instrument that excites them.
Alexis de Tocqueville
Democracy in America, Vol. II, II, 8

I T'S TRUE THAT much of the cooperation among people is based on mutual satisfaction of needs and desires. We're willing to help other people if they're willing to help us. This is one of the main supports of community. We have similar needs, and we can best meet them if we help each other. But if I don't want your help, am I free to ignore you or even mistreat you?

Maybe I have no itch, or I think I can find another way to get my back scratched. Am I then free to refuse to help you? Or maybe I'm so confident in my power to make you meet my needs that I'll just take from you and give nothing back. Is there any reason why I shouldn't, if I can get away with it?

There's nothing wrong with helping each other out of mutual self-interest. Much of our daily life is spent in such activities. It's the basis for capitalism: I'll invest in what you're doing so long as I'll also gain from my investment. It's the basis for a lot of political compromise. One side gives the other something it wants and then gets something valuable in return.

But is such a system of mutual self-interest enough? Don't people deserve to be helped for their own sakes? Do you think others should be good to you only if they gain from it? To agree to this is to see yourself as expendable, as merely a means to satisfy the desires of others. But you deserve to be treated with dignity and respect. So does every human being.

> It's good that all backs get scratched, even
> if out of mutual self-interest. But it's far better
> to help each other because we see that each
> person is worthy of respect and compassion.

Everyone should help others so far as he can. The goals of every person should also be my goals if my actions are really to be in full harmony with the idea that every person's humanity is an end in itself.
Immanuel Kant
Foundations of the Metaphysics of Morals, II

Persons Quoted

Henry Adams (1838-1918), American historian

Conrad Aiken (1889-1973), American poet, writer

St. Anselm (1033-1109), Scholastic philosopher and theologian

St. Thomas Aquinas (c. 1225-1274), Dominican philosopher and theologian

Aristotle (384-322 B.C.), Greek philosopher

W. H. Auden (1907-1973), English poet

St. Augustine (354-430), philosopher and theologian, Bishop of Hippo

Francis Bacon (1561-1626), British philosopher, essayist, and statesman

Lawrence Batler (20th century), American psychologist and author

Francis Beaumont (1584-1616), British playwright

Ruth Benedict (1887-1948), American anthropologist

Robert Hugh Benson (1871-1914), British author, Catholic priest

Jeremy Bentham (1748-1832), British philosopher, jurist, and social reformer

Cyrano de Bergerac (1619-1655), French satirist, playwright

Henri Bergson (1859-1941) French philosopher

Claude Bernard (1813-1878), French physiologist

Boethius (c. 480-524), Christian philosopher and theologian

Sir Thomas Browne (1605-1682), British writer, physician

Jimmy Carter (b. 1924), 39th President of the United States

Sébastien Roch Nicolas Chamfort (1741-1794), French writer

John Bryson Chane (b. 1945) American Episcopal Bishop of Washington, DC

Geoffrey Chaucer (c. 1343-1400), British poet

G. K. Chesterton (1874-1936), British essayist, novelist, and philosopher

Winston Churchill (1874-1965), British statesman and author

Cicero (106-43 B.C.), Roman statesman, orator, and philosopher

W. K. Clifford (1845-1879), British philosopher

Barbara Coloroso (b. 1947), American author, educator

Auguste Comte (1798-1857), French philosopher, sociologist

Laurent A. Daloz (20th century), American educator

LEONARDO DA VINCI (1452-1519), Italian painter, sculptor, inventor

JOHN DEWEY (1859-1952), American philosopher and educator

JOHN DRYDEN (1631-1700), British Poet Laureate

ALBERT EINSTEIN (1879-1955), American physicist

RALPH WALDO EMERSON (1803-1882), American author, minister, activist

EURIPIDES (c. 480-406 B.C.), Greek tragic playwright

JOHN FINNIS (b. 1940), British moral philosopher

EDWARD FITZGERALD (1809-1883), British scholar and poet

JOHN FLETCHER (1579-1625), British playwright

ANATOLE FRANCE (1844-1924), French writer, novelist, Nobel Prize winner

EDWARD GIBBON (1737-1794), British historian

JOHANN WOLFGANG VON GOETHE (1749-1832), German poet and dramatist

EDMOND DE GONCOURT (1822-1896), French novelist

JULES DE GONCOURT (1830-1870), French novelist

ST. GREGORY I (THE GREAT) (540-604), a Father of the Church

JOHN B. S. HALDANE (1892-1964), British biologist, geneticist, author

WILLIAM HAZLITT (1778-1830) British essayist

LILLIAN HELLMAN (1905-1984), American playwright

JOHN HEYWOOD (c. 1575), British playwright and musician

ADOLF HITLER (1889-1945), German dictator

HORACE (65-8 B.C.), Latin poet, satirist

VICTOR HUGO (1802-1885), French author

DAVID HUME (1711-1776), British philosopher

HENRY JAMES (1843-1916) American writer, novelist

WILLIAM JAMES (1842-1910), American philosopher, psychologist

THOMAS JEFFERSON (1743-1826), 3rd president of the United States

SAMUEL JOHNSON (1709-1784), British lexicographer, writer

IMMANUEL KANT (1724-1804), German philosopher

THOMAS À KEMPIS (c. 1380-1471), German Christian ascetical writer

MARTIN LUTHER KING, JR. (1929-1968), American civil rights leader

C. S. LEWIS (1898-1963), British writer and philosopher

Georg Christoph Lichtenberg (1742-1799), German mathematician

Abraham Lincoln (1809-1865), 16th American president

Lucretius (c. 50 B.C.), Roman poet and philosopher

Joseph de Maistre (1753-1821), French diplomat, philosopher

Jacques Maritain (1882-1973), French philosopher

St. Matthew (1st century), Christian Apostle and evangelist

Mary McCarthy (1912-1989), American writer, satirist, journalist

Michel de Montaigne (1533-1592), French essayist and philosopher

Montesquieu (1689-1755), French philosopher and jurist

Lewis Mumford (1895-1990), American social thinker, writer

Dame Iris Murdoch (1919-1999), British novelist and philosopher

Kent Nerburn (b. 1946), American author, sculptor, and educator

St. Philip Neri (1515-1595) Italian Catholic priest, mystic, saint

Isaac Newton (1643-1727), British physicist and mathematician

Friedrich Wilhelm Nietzsche (1844-1900), German philosopher

Henry Old Coyote (c. 1912-1988), American educator

Blaise Pascal (1623-1662), French mathematician and philosopher

Walter Pater (1839-1894), British critic, essayist

Thomas Love Peacock (1785-1866), British novelist and poet

Charles Sanders Peirce (1839-1914), American philosopher, mathematician

Plato (c. 427-347 B.C.), Greek philosopher

Protagoras (c. 490-421 B.C.), Greek philosopher

Anna Quindlen (b. 1953), American journalist, 1992 Pulitzer Prize winner

Quintilian (c. 100), Roman rhetorician

Ayn Rand (1905-1982), American novelist, philosopher

Agnes Repplier (1855-1950), American essayist

Dorothy Rich (b. 1932), American author, educator

Franklin D. Roosevelt (1882-1945), 32nd president of the United States

Harold Rosenberg (1906-1978), American author, critic

Jean-Jacques Rousseau (1712-1778), French political philosopher, writer

John Ruskin (1819-1900), British writer, art critic, and social reformer

Jean-Paul Sartre (1905-1980), French Existentialist philosopher, writer

Arthur Schopenhauer (1788-1860), German philosopher

Carl Schurz (1829-1906), American senator and Civil War general

William Shakespeare (1564-1616), British poet and dramatist

George Bernard Shaw (1856-1950), British playwright and novelist

Christopher Smart (1722-1771), British poet

Adam Smith (1723-1790), British economist and moral philosopher

Socrates (c. 470-399 B.C.), Athenian philosopher and teacher

Solon (c. 550 B.C.), Athenian statesman, lawgiver, poet

John Lancaster Spalding (1840-1916), American Catholic Bishop

Bruce Springsteen (b. 1949), American singer, songwriter, guitarist

Thomas Szasz (b. 1920), American psychiatrist, author

Jeremy Taylor (1613-1667), British theologian

Alfred Lord Tennyson (1809-1892) British poet

Theophilus (c. 385), Patriarch of Alexandria

Thucydides (c. 460-400 B.C.), Athenian historian

Alexis de Tocqueville (1805-1859), French author, statesman

William Ullathorne (1806-1889), British Benedictine, Archbishop of Cabasa

Peter Ustinov (b. 1921), British actor and playwright

Oscar Wilde (1854-1900), British poet, playwright, novelist, critic

Virginia Woolf (1882-1941), British author

Frances Wright (1795-1852), Scottish-born American abolitionist and author

Biographical Note

Montague Brown

After he completed his undergraduate degree in English Literature at the University of California at Berkeley in 1978, Montague Brown's wife gave him a copy of *The Collected Dialogues of Plato*. Plato's quest for truth and all-encompassing intellectual honesty soon had Brown hooked on philosophy.

Brown moved on from Plato to devour the works of Aristotle, Augustine, and Aquinas. After avidly reading the entire text of Aquinas's more than 2,000-page *Summa Theologica*, he decided to undertake the formal study of philosophy and received a Ph.D. in philosophy from Boston College in 1986.

Literature and its real-life preoccupations — such as the questions addressed here in *Half-Truths* — have always loomed large in Dr. Brown's philosophical work. He has served as chair of the Commission on the Arts at St. Anselm College in New Hampshire, where he teaches courses involving John Milton's *Paradise Lost* and Dante's *Commedia.* Dr. Brown has lectured on everything from *Antigone* and *Hamlet* to *Zen and the Art of Motorcycle Maintenance.*

He is the author of *The Romance of Reason: An Adventure in the Thought of Thomas Aquinas* plus a matter-of-fact ethics book called *The Quest for Moral Foundations*. His most recent book is *The One-Minute Philosopher.*

An amiable raconteur and an accomplished bassist — as well as a professor of philosophy at St. Anselm College for more than seventeen years — Dr. Brown lives in Weare, New Hampshire, with his wife, Meeta, and their four children.

Sophia Institute

Sophia Institute is a nonprofit institution that seeks to nurture the spiritual, moral, and cultural life of souls and to spread the Gospel of Christ in conformity with the authentic teachings of the Roman Catholic Church.

Sophia Institute Press fulfills this mission by offering translations, reprints, and new publications that afford readers a rich source of the enduring wisdom of mankind.

Sophia Institute also operates two popular online Catholic resources: CrisisMagazine.com and CatholicExchange.com.

Crisis Magazine provides insightful cultural analysis that arms readers with the arguments necessary for navigating the ideological and theological minefields of the day. *Catholic Exchange* provides world news from a Catholic perspective as well as daily devotionals and articles that will help you to grow in holiness and live a life consistent with the teachings of the Church.

In 2013, Sophia Institute launched Sophia Institute for Teachers to renew and rebuild Catholic culture through service to Catholic education. With the goal of nurturing the spiritual, moral, and cultural life of souls, and an abiding respect for the role and work of teachers, we strive to provide materials and programs that are at once enlightening to the mind and ennobling to the heart; faithful and complete, as well as useful and practical.

Sophia Institute gratefully recognizes the Solidarity Association for preserving and encouraging the growth of our apostolate over the course of many years. Without their generous and timely support, this book would not be in your hands.

www.SophiaInstitute.com
www.CatholicExchange.com
www.CrisisMagazine.com
www.SophiaInstituteforTeachers.org